W9-BKV-392

A2180 155716 1

DATE DUE		
Apr. 19, 2005		

OVERDUE FINE
$0.10 PER DAY

CHOCOLATE

THE NATURE OF INDULGENCE

Ruth Lopez

WOODBRIDGE TOWN LIBRARY
10 NEWTON ROAD
WOODBRIDGE CT 06525

HARRY N. ABRAMS, INC., PUBLISHERS
IN ASSOCIATION WITH THE FIELD MUSEUM

CONTENTS

INTRODUCTION

Food of the gods. An Aztec ruler hands the sea god Neptune a box of chocolates to be distributed throughout the world on his aquatic chariot. From a book in Latin on chocolate, published in 1639.

In 1753, the Swedish botanist Carl von Linné (better known as Carolus Linnaeus) assigned the binomial classification *Theobroma cacao* to the tree from whose seeds chocolate is made. The word *Theobroma* was an interesting choice, coming as it does from the Greek for "food of the gods." Linnaeus may have had his own reasons for picking the term; he was a deeply religious man who believed that understanding God's wisdom could come only by studying His creation. But *Theobroma* is meaningful on other levels, for chocolate was a sacred substance for the people of pre-Columbian America, and even today it seems to have an almost spiritual appeal for those who find the taste of chocolate irresistible.

What we taste when we consume a piece of well-made chocolate is actually hundreds of different substances present in the cacao seed, and try as they might, chemists have been unable to manufacture a decent synthetic substitute. This fact makes *Theobroma cacao* as much a precious resource today as it was when it was first discovered in Mesoamerica, long before the arrival of Europeans.

The manufacture of chocolate candy is today a very big business in the United States, but the essential ingredient did not come to North America directly from its southern neighbors. The secret of the cacao bean had been discovered long before the Spanish conquest in the sixteenth century, but it was only after the Aztec recipe for chocolate was refined in Europe that chocolate became an international delicacy and ultimately a world commodity, with plantations as far flung as Ivory Coast and Indonesia and products ranging from premium artisanal chocolate to mass-produced candy bars.

It is a long way from the rainforest to the candy counter, but the story of how chocolate got from one place to the other is a fascinating tale—as complex as chocolate's flavor—and one that enhances our appreciation of the important role that chocolate may have to play not only in its own survival but also in the preservation of its original environment. Like other natives of the rainforest—coffee, rubber, mangos, and many species of nuts—cacao has an uncertain future, for its natural habitat is increasingly threatened with deforestation, whether by farming, grazing, logging, or mining.

A true understanding of chocolate involves an awareness of numerous disciplines, including archaeology, botany, conservation biology, cultural anthropology, and economics. In the process of gathering materials for this book, traces of chocolate were found almost everywhere, from cookbooks to medical treatises and books about colonialism, the slave trade, and the history of Mexico. Because we can offer here only bite-size pieces of information, we recommend that you consult the bibliography at the back of this book, where you will find a world of sources to explore.

One does not need a book to appreciate the flavor of fine chocolate, but that flavor is significantly enhanced by the knowledge that one seed from one pod of a tree growing deep in the forest has such phenomenal power. Not only does the taste derived from that seed appeal to millions of people throughout the world, but the story of how that taste became so widespread gives us a unique opportunity to examine so many different aspects of our own culture, the most important of which may be our own relationship to the world around us.

"They are not at all beautiful, nor so agreeable to the Eye, as the Fruit is to the Palate of them that love Chocolatto."

FROM *Philosophical Transactions: An accurate description of the Cacao-tree, and the way of its curing and husbandry, given by an Intelligent Person now residing in Jamaica* (1673)

Turning Trees into Chocolate

The Forest

The lush, tropical rainforest is home to the cacao tree. But the rainforest is more than just a place where chocolate comes from—it is the only environment in which this tree thrives. The tropical belt extends about 20 degrees north and 20 degrees south along the equator, and its forests are the most biologically diverse in the world, places where plants and animals have adapted to unique climatic conditions by cycling their nutrients in a complex and very efficient system. The largest expanse of tropical forest on earth is in the Americas, stretching from the Gulf Coast of Mexico down to the Amazon and Orinoco basins of Brazil and Venezuela.

The rainforest is an intricate and fragile ecosystem, and disturbance of any element in it can wreak havoc on the whole. The sun, which rises to a nearly vertical position every day at noon provides a high level of radiant energy throughout the year. The hot, humid air continually rises and condenses, resulting in eighty to four hundred inches of rainfall annually, with temperatures averaging 80 degrees F. This year-round climate creates a productive

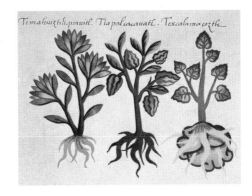

The earliest-known image of a cacao tree is the middle drawing in this illustration from the Badianus Manuscript, an Aztec herbal composed in 1552 by Martin de la Cruz and Juannes Badianus, Aztec students at the College of Santa Cruz at Tlaltelco, Mexico City.

OPPOSITE A view of the rainforest in Costa Rica, where cacao grows wild

The rainforest canopy provides crucial shade for the cacao tree.

Cacao is only one of the many products of the rainforest.

environment; a healthy rainforest can produce ten to twelve tons of new growth per acre annually, twice as much as a temperate forest.

The tallest trees in the rainforest, which can attain heights of up to 130 feet, form what is called an upper canopy, which absorbs as much as 90 percent of the sunlight that falls on the forest. The lower levels remain relatively dark, although temperatures there can reach 96 degrees with a humidity of at least 60 percent. The trees in the understory range from 65 to 100 feet tall, and they provide homes for butterflies and arborial mammals such as monkeys and three-toed sloths, who rarely descend to the ground. Very little light filters down through the canopy, perhaps as little as 1 to 2 percent of the sun's intensity, so not much grows on the forest floor. Temperatures there average about 82 degrees, but the humidity can rise to 90 percent, creating a rich environment for decaying vegetation such as dead trees and fallen leaves, on which insects, fungi, and other creatures thrive.

It is in the understory of the humid lowland tropics (below 1,000 feet in altitude) where the cacao tree lives. *Theobroma cacao,* which in the wild can reach a height of 30 to 40 feet, lives in the shade of the larger trees, protected from the sun and wind and nourished by the moisture that trickles down. Many other plants do well in this environment; in fact, at least 80 percent of the foods used by the developed world originated in the tropical rainforest, whose gifts include fruits: avocados, coconuts, figs, oranges, lemons, grapefruit, bananas, guavas, pineapples, mangos, and tomatoes; vegetables: corn (maize), potatoes, rice, winter squash, and yams; spices: black pepper, cayenne, cinnamon, cloves, ginger, sugar cane, turmeric, vanilla; Brazil nuts and cashews; and medications: quinine, curare, annatto, and many more.

It is difficult to imagine life without these staple foods, and yet we seem to have lost interest in the rainforests from which they came. Although scientists have provided evidence that the rainforest contributes significantly to the health and well-being of the rest of the world by continuously recycling carbon dioxide into oxygen, politicians and corporate leaders have been slow to recognize that sacrificing rainforest for agricultural expansion will have a disastrous effect far beyond the forest. Rainforests once covered 14 percent of the earth's land surface, but now they cover only about 7 percent. At the current rate of deforestation, scientists estimate that they may all be gone in forty years.

The Tree

Theobroma cacao most likely evolved as a wild tree in South America, in the upper Orinoco River region of Venezuela or in the Amazon basin of Brazil. Scientists have never been able to agree upon the exact point, or points, of its origin or to explain how the tree managed to migrate north into Central America. Interestingly, the people of Amazonia learned to domesticate cacao, not for chocolate but for the sweet pulp that surrounds the cacao seeds.

Theobroma cacao is a member of the family of tropical plants known as Sterculiaceae, which also includes its distant relative the cola tree, a primary source of the flavoring used to make soft drinks, another product that has achieved a dominant position in both popular culture and gastronomy. According to scientists, *T. cacao* is a relatively recent species, dating back ten to fifteen thousand years, while its genus, *Theobroma,* has been around for many millions of years. Twenty-two species of *Theobroma* were identified in 1964 by the Mexican botanist José Cuatrecasas, but only two of them produce the

The cacao tree and its taller "mother" tree in Tabasco, Mexico

Cacao flowers attract midges, which pollinate the tree.

An opened cacao pod, showing the sweet pulp and the seeds inside

fruit we care about, *T. cacao* and *T. bicolor*. The latter is not a good source of cacao, as Robert Whymper wrote in a 1921 book on cacao cultivation: "No one seems to have a good word for *T. bicolor,* called 'Tiger cacao' from the rank smell of its seeds." Still, it has been an important garden crop in Central and South America, and the pulp is used to make Nicaragua's national beverage, *pinolillo.*

Theobroma cacao is an odd-looking tree whose football-shaped fruit, the pods, grow directly out of the trunk and branches rather than at the tips, as with many other fruits. Before the era of photography, those who did not know the tree assumed that botanical drawings made by naturalists were the result of faulty artistry. One observer defended an artist's work in 1891 explaining that the drawing was "in fact a rude expression of one of the most remarkable peculiarities of the plant." Another early reporter went to convoluted lengths to describe the pod as "irregular and angular, much like some forms of cucumbers, but more pointed at the lower extremity, and more distinctly grooved." Which is to say, the cacao pod would look just like a cucumber if a cucumber were shaped more like a football.

The species *T. cacao* comprises several different varieties. The original tree encountered by the Spanish in Mexico is called *criollo* (Spanish for native-born) and it is still cultivated in South America (as well as Indonesia), although very little is now grown in Mexico. The elongated criollo pods are not very hardy and produce few beans, but they are used to make premium chocolate. *Forastero* (meaning foreign) is native to the upper Amazon region; it yields more pods per tree and its aromatic beans are higher in tannin content. This has become the most widely cultivated variety, especially in Africa, which produces most of the world's cacao today. *Trinitario,* which was developed in Trinidad and is now grown in Cameroon and Papua New Guinea, is a hybrid of the first two varieties, and its qualities are closest to those of the forastero. According to a report issued in 1891 by the Walter Baker Company in Massachusetts, then the largest chocolate maker in America, the two varieties of the cocoa tree cultivated in Venezuela were known as "El Criollo and El Trinitario, the former of which, though not so prolific…is considered superior in size, color, sweetness, and oleaginous properties."

Cacao leaves

Although the cacao tree obtains protection and moisture from the taller trees in the upper canopy, it absorbs nutrients from the rainforest floor, including nitrogen released by the decaying vegetation. *T. cacao* also owes much to the tiny insects, or midges, that breed in the humus of the forest floor. Attracted to the scent of the tiny pink flowers that grow in clusters along the tree's branches and trunk, these midges pollinate the blossoms as they take in nectar. Each pollinated blossom will grow into an elongated pod that houses the seeds, or beans, used to make the substance we know as chocolate.

Cacao seeds are also what produces new trees. Because the pods do not naturally fall to the forest floor when they are ripe, the tree must rely on monkeys, bats, and other animals with a taste for sweet cacao pulp to gnaw through the tough pod coverings and release the bitter seeds. Once the seeds reach the ground, they germinate, and new trees begin to grow. Like most plants in this warm, moist environment, the cacao tree grows quickly, but it does not produce a crop of pods until its fifth year.

A cacao tree in its prime will yield about fifty pods twice a year, as it takes five to six months for a pod to ripen. The pods can grow up to twelve inches in length and five inches in diameter at the mid-section, turning from green to

Ripening cacao pods

"Within this pucaminious husk or large fruit, ly the Cacahuatl or (as the Spaniards corruptly call them) the Cacao nuts, being about the bigness of Almonds, each of them enveloped in a slimy substance, and film, of a Phlegmatique complexion, but of a most refreshing taste: which women love to suck of from the Cacao, finding it cool, and in the mouth dissolving into water."

HENRY STUBBE,
The Indian Nectar (1662)

brilliant shades of red, yellow, and orange as they mature. Housed in each sturdy pod are about forty almond-sized seeds encased in a sweet, moist pulp, enough to make about ten milk chocolate bars or four candy bars of dark chocolate.

The people of Mesoamerica considered cacao a gift from nature that provided a substance they found nourishing both physically and spiritually. To meet the demand, the earliest users of the aromatic cacao seeds developed methods of cultivating the wild tree. The Olmec, who lived along the Gulf of Mexico as early as 1500 B.C., in what are now the states of Tabasco and Veracruz, are believed to have grown cacao trees at the edge of the rainforest, creating small gardens that also provided other foods, such as corn, tomatoes, and vanilla. The Maya in the Yucatan peninsula grew trees in deep natural wells called *cenotes,* and created irrigation canals in small shady groves. Surrounded by taller trees, *T. cacao* thrived in these well-drained hollows, which always had ground water circulating through them to create a dependable source of moisture. Since the orchards were far apart, they did not harbor pests and plant diseases, and yet they provided a good environment for the pollinating insects. The Maya also developed a trade network and transported cacao into drier regions where it could not be grown.

Other early cultivators of cacao include the indigenous peoples of Costa Rica, who were able to grow the tree along densely shaded riverbanks. The premier cacao-producing region for the Aztecs was Soconusco in Chiapas, a Mexican state near the border of Guatemala. Like the Maya, the Aztecs also maintained extensive trade routes, bringing from the tropical south various products that were valued in the dry central Mexican plateau, including precious feathers, gold, jade, and cacao.

We know more about *T. cacao* as a cultivated crop than as a wild rainforest tree. As Allen M. Young wrote in his 1994 book, *The Chocolate Tree: A Natural History of Cacao:* "The extent to which *T. cacao* was dispersed outward from its center of origin in Amazonia by natural means (such as seed released by animals from the tree's pods and the movement of seeds along streams and rivers) or by prehistoric peoples cannot be ascertained at this time." There are, however, many theories as to how cacao was dispersed and how it might have been carried across the Andes, where the seeds would not have survived the cold. In

A cacao tree with ripening pods

recent years, some botanists claim to have discovered wild cacao populations in the Lakandon rainforest in Chiapas, although whether they originated in the area or somehow migrated from South America is still open to question.

Scientists generally agree that the sweet cacao pulp must have been what initially attracted natives of South America to the tree. Allen Young suggests that it was natural human curiosity about the weird-looking pods jutting out from the trunk and branches that led to the discovery of chocolate. Those initial investigations probably began with a cracked pod and a tentative taste of juicy pulp, and from there one can imagine a scenario in which the bitter seeds, discarded into a fire pit, began to release the seductive chocolate aroma that continues to cast its spell today.

OPPOSITE This image of a cacao tree growing in a Maya *cenote,* or well, was taken from a painted capstone of the Temple of the Owls.

Although most cacao is now produced in Africa, *T. cacao* still grows in the lowlands of Chiapas and Tabasco, where, as chocolate expert Elaine González writes, it continues to be considered a sacred crop. "Today there are many countries that lie within twenty degrees of the equator that grow and sell cacao to the world market, but few of them have any cultural connection with it."

Although cacao has been widely cultivated on large plantations in various regions around the world, farmers have discovered over the years that cacao grows best when it is grown in its natural habitat. They have learned this seemingly obvious fact the hard way. An early and crucial observation was that the cacao tree does best when shade is available, although this has not stopped many planters from attempting to grow cacao without a protective canopy. These efforts are not unsuccessful, but the trees are relatively

A cacao nursery in Bolivia, where cacao trees are cultivated outside the rainforest

short-lived (up to ten years), produce fewer pods than their wild counterparts, and are more susceptible to disease. Farmers are reluctant to invest in large shade trees that hold little or no economic value, so they turn to species that provides a commercial incentive as producers of castor oil, bananas, and rubber.

A 1900 agricultural manual for growing cacao described the ideal spot to start a plantation: "a well-sheltered vale, covered with large trees, protected by mountain spurs from the prevailing winds, well watered, and yet well drained, with a good depth of alluvial soil, on which rests a thick deposit of decayed vegetable matter, easy of access, and in a district distant from lagoons or marshes, for the sake of the proprietor's health. Such a spot in a climate similar to that of Trinidad could not fail to produce regular crops of the finest quality of cacao."

By far the most serious problem for cacao growers, however, has been the tree's susceptibility to pests and plant diseases such as pod rot and types of fungus, especially for trees that grow outside the rainforest. From the very beginning, European growers with plantations in the Caribbean complained about uneven harvests caused by disease, insects, or bad weather, and in fact, obtaining satisfactory yields from cacao plantations has always been a challenge. For decades, the cacao industry could escape the problem by planting trees in new areas of rainforest in other parts of the world, but as tropical rainforests decline, the planters are running out of places to go.

Over time, cacao growers have come to understand all of the factors necessary to cultivating healthy *Theobroma cacao*. It has always been known that cacao trees thrive in the moist soil and humid conditions, but large-scale commercial cultivation has not been able to duplicate all the benefits the rainforest gives to cacao trees, especially the function of pollination. The two types of midges that are most attracted to cacao flowers—ceratopogonid midges and gall midges of the family Diptera—thrive under the rainforest canopy, where they are protected from strong winds and where the moist debris on the ground provides ideal breeding conditions. It may be for reasons of natural pollination that the plantations located on the edge of rainforests produce higher yields than plantations in areas established away from them, no matter how carefully conditions may be imitated.

Cacao beans

The cacao bean contains about three hundred substances that affect the flavor and nutritional value of chocolate, including antioxidants, stearic acid, copper, magnesium, calcium, and caffeine.

This rainforest midge, responsible for pollinating the cacao tree, is much smaller than it appears in this photograph.

Scientists are now reexamining the way in which Mesoamerican peoples cultivated cacao on the borders of the rainforest or in small orchards within the forest. There seems to be a new consensus that a return to the ancient way of growing cacao is worth the effort. By preserving a system of agriculture that has been around for thousands of years, cacao and the people who grow it can be assured of a future and can in turn help the rainforest remain intact.

The Bean

In his 1892 book, *Cocoa: All About It,* the English chocolate manufacturer Richard Cadbury, writing under the pseudonym Historicus, described the beauty of a cacao plantation ready for harvest. "The branches do not grow low, so that in looking from the ground the vista is like a miniature forest hung with thousands of golden lamps—anything more lovely cannot be imagined."

A plantation worker opening a cacao pod with his machete

Cacao beans fermenting in the Dominican Republic

It is likely that Cadbury's affection for this scene was enhanced by the value of the pods, called black gold (*oro negro*) by the Spanish. Even today people in Ecuador still call cacao seeds *pepe de oro,* "seeds of gold."

It is also likely that Cadbury's workers, many of whom undoubtedly descended from slaves, did not find much beauty in this sight. Harvesting cacao is hard work, and it has not changed much over the years. The pods are still cut from tree with machetes, skillfully maneuvered so as not to damage the flowers or the flower "cushions" on which they grow. Within a day or two after harvesting, the pods must be split so that the seeds, or beans, may be removed by hand along with the slippery pulp. The pod husks are often left in piles to collect rainwater and to create breeding grounds for potential pollinators, and the beans and pulp are prepared for fermentation. Exposure to the air transforms the color of the beans from purple to the deep brown we associate with chocolate, but they do not yet resemble or smell like it.

Cacao pods

Raking beans to dry

OPPOSITE Oven for roasting cacao beans

The wet beans and pulp are placed in sacks, in large wooden boxes or barrels covered with plantain leaves, or in special buildings, to undergo the process of fermentation, "upon which, in a great measure, the commercial value of Cocoa depends," according to Historicus (Cadbury). The beans and pulp are allowed to "sweat," or ferment, for an average of four to seven days, depending on the variety of the bean or the quality of the chocolate desired. The longer the process, the better the flavor (and the higher the cost); premium chocolate requires more than ten days, according to some chocolate makers. During fermentation, yeasts and bacteria fed by the pulp increase the temperature of the beans, and this heat causes a chemical change in which the natural sugars are converted to lactic and acetic acid. The heat also activates enzymes in the beans to form compounds that will produce the flavor of chocolate after roasting and expels the bitter flavor of the beans.

After fermentation, the beans (now loosened from the pulp) are spread out to dry in the sun for about a week. Every few days, they are raked and turned over until they contain only about 5 percent water, a level low enough to keep fungus from growing during shipping. This is the point at which chocolate-to-be is packed in sacks and transported to factories where the beans will undergo further processing, necessary steps in the alchemy that will result in black gold.

The Cocoa

After fermentation and drying, the cacao beans are roasted, a delicate process that ultimately determines the flavor and color of the resulting chocolate. After roasting, the Maya would remove the husks and pound the kernels, or nibs, with stones, called *manos,* against a stone surface, or *metate,* under which fires were often built to facilitate the process. After the kernels were crushed, the resulting paste was hardened into solid chunks, which would then be broken up, mixed with water and various seasonings, and heated. The heat caused a fatty substance to rise to the surface, where it would be skimmed off. Some of this fat was returned to the liquid, which would be poured back and forth between two pots, one held high above the other, to

Mexican woman grinding cacao beans with a
metate

Cakes of cocoa powder at a factory in Tabasco,
Mexico

emulsify the fat and create a frothy drink that was considered a delicacy (see Chapter 2).

Although the harvesting and preparation of cacao beans has not really changed over the years, the making of chocolate went through some major changes during the nineteenth century, as chocolate became more popular, both as a drink and later as a food, and manufacturing techniques became more efficient and sophisticated. The first major invention, that of the cacao press in 1828 by the Dutch chocolate maker Coenraad Van Houten, was quickly adopted by manufacturers and permanently changed the way in which chocolate was made. Instead of being crushed by hand, the nibs are ground by a machine that produces enough frictional heat to liquefy the fatty substance, or cocoa butter, which makes up about 55 percent of the crushed nibs, or "cocoa liquor" (this term does not indicate alcohol, only liquid). Some of the cocoa butter is then removed from the liquor, and the remaining chocolate is poured into molds, where it solidifies into unsweetened, or bitter, cakes that can be pulverized into the powder we call cocoa.

Cacao pod with a drink made from the pulp

Processing cacao beans at a plantation in the West Indies

The extracted cocoa butter, which can be stored as a solid for long periods of time but melts at about 90 degrees F., plays a very important part in the manufacture of eating chocolate. Modern manufacturers return a certain amount of the cocoa butter to the cocoa and mix it until the fat is emulsified and the mixture is smooth. Conching, a technique developed in Switzerland in the nineteenth century, is a process in which machines (originally shaped like conch shells) knead the chocolate mixture to remove even the finest grains of cocoa to make the chocolate very smooth and to develop flavor. In order to prevent the cocoa butter from crystallizing and affecting the appearance and texture of the chocolate, some manufacturers put it through yet another process, called tempering, in which the chocolate mixture is heated to about 150 degrees F. and cooled. Although chocolate is sometimes shipped in liquid

Workers in the Menier chocolate factory near Paris

The manufacture of chocolate, France, c. 1900

form, usually it is molded into large bars to be shipped to distributors, confectioners, and other manufacturers who use chocolate in creating their products.

It is ironic that, as the market for chocolate continues to grow and the refinement of manufacturing techniques continues to improve, the places where cacao comes from are beginning to shrink. It is encouraging that scientists, farmers, and grass-roots organizations, as well as chocolate manufacturers, are looking at cacao's past in order to plan for chocolate's future.

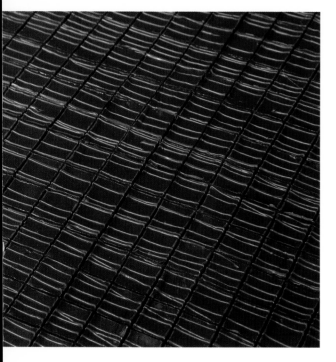

"I am aware that people of feeble imagination will accuse me of being fantastic when I speak of trees bearing money."

Peter Martyr D'Anghiera, *De Orbe Novo* (1530)

The Drink of the Gods

Before the Spanish conquest in 1521, ancient Mesoamerica extended from what is now Costa Rica in the south to north-central Mexico, and was bordered on the west coast by the Pacific Ocean, on the east coast by the Caribbean Sea, and on the north by the Gulf of Mexico. Many extraordinary ancient societies flourished here, beginning at least as early as 1500 B.C. with the Olmec, followed by, among others, the Maya, Zapotec, Mixtec, Toltec, and Aztec peoples. When the Europeans arrived, the Aztecs ruled the Valley of Mexico, where their capital city, Tenochtitlán, stood on an island, now the site of Mexico City. It was here that the Spanish got their first taste of chocolate.

Much of what we know about life in Mesoamerica is based on what the Spanish observed in sixteenth-century Aztec society, whose customs incorporated many elements from the traditions and beliefs of earlier cultures. A clearer, more detailed picture of life before the conquest, however, continues to emerge as archaeologists and scholars decipher and interpret the material remains of the brilliant civilizations that preceded the Aztecs. The Maya, who had flourished in Mesoamerica since at least 300 B.C. and reached their peak between A.D. 240 and 900, still inhabited the Yucatán peninsula and parts of

This ancient Maya statue was found in Guatemala. It is decorated with clay cacao seeds and may have been used to offer cacao to the gods.

OPPOSITE A European drawing of an Aztec woman making chocolate by pouring the beverage from one pot into another to blend the ingredients

29

Sor Juana Inés de la Cruz, the great Mexican poet nun of the seventeenth century, sent a poem along with a gift of ground chocolate and an embroidered shoe to her patroness, the countess of Galve. The poem declares that its message is held in secret by the turns of the molinillo. ("Hasta el recado tasado/va, tan mudo y sin ruido,/que van guardando secreto/las ruedas del molinillo.") Sor Juana was well aware of the hard labor involved in preparing chocolate. When a man referred to her as the elusive phoenix of antiquity, the poetess responded with great humor; she was glad she was no longer a woman, as it meant that, among all the chores expected of her, she would not have to grind chocolate.

Central America at the time of the conquest. Their accomplishments were great, especially in agriculture and architecture, but perhaps most remarkable was the strong tradition of picture, or hieroglyphic, writing, which enabled them to document their beliefs, events, and customs in manuscript form and on ceramic vessels, stone monuments, and wall paintings. It is in these ancient writings that scholars have found evidence of the significance of chocolate in Mesoamerican life.

Unfortunately, only a few of the codices, as the richly illustrated pre-Columbian texts are known, survived the widespread book-burning practices carried out by the Spanish clergy, but those that exist today, most of them scattered in European libraries, are invaluable sources of information about the culture of early Mexico. The Dresden Codex, for example, contains Maya astronomical calculations; the Paris Codex is devoted almost entirely to Maya ritual and ceremony; and the Madrid Codex contains information about astrology and divinatory practices. Of particular interest to us is an illustration in the Codex Mendoza, in which two hundred loads of cacao beans and containers of chocolate are seen included in the tribute collected by the Aztecs from the cacao-rich region of Soconusco. This codex is named for a Spanish viceroy who commissioned Aztec scribes to compile texts and images in 1541 in order to inform King Charles V about his new subjects.

Archaeological finds are another important source of information about the earliest ways in which chocolate was used in the region. For many years, scholars credited the Maya with discovering the wonders of chocolate. In El Salvador, for example, the Maya village of Cerén, which was buried under more than ten feet of ash from a volcanic eruption in A.D. 590, has yielded dishes full of cacao seeds and the remains of cultivated cacao trees. Some archaeologists now believe, however, that the first use of chocolate dates even further back, perhaps to the Olmec, who lived along the Gulf Coast of Mexico from 1500 to 400 B.C. Anthropologist Michael Coe is the primary proponent of this idea and bases his evidence, admittedly slim, on the assumption that the word *cacao* appears to have originated in the Mixe-Zoquen language family used by the Olmec.

Recently, scientists from Cornell University and the University of California at Berkeley found evidence of an even older society, which occupied a

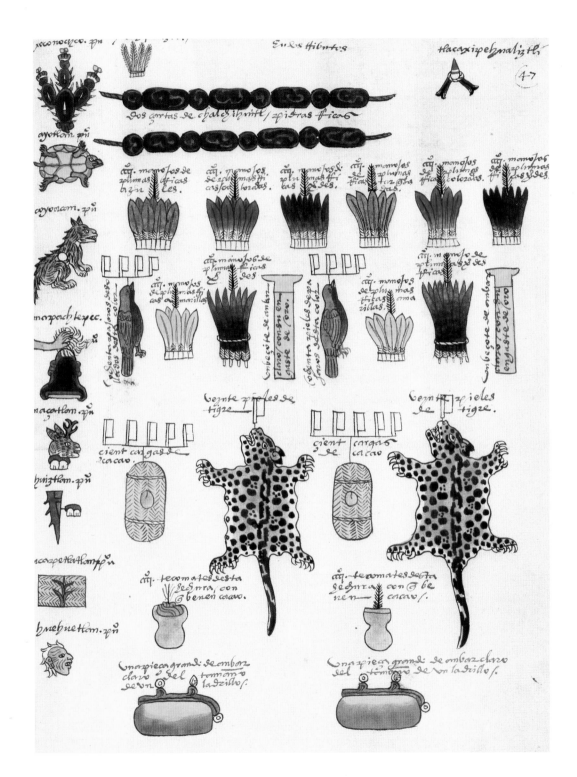

Aztec rulers required conquered subjects to pay a tax, or tribute, and those who lived in cacao-growing areas paid in cacao beans. This image, from the sixteenth-century Codex Mendoza, created by Aztec scribes for their Spanish captors, shows a pictorial list of goods presented to the Aztecs. Below the ocelot skins are gourds used for drinking cacao. To the left of the skins are sacks containing cacao beans.

This rollout shows the image painted on the so-called Princeton vase, which dates to the eighth century and depicts a woman holding a jar from which she pours a dark substance into a larger jar at her feet, perhaps the oldest image of chocolate preparation.

Honduran village continuously from B.C. 2000 to A.D. 1000. The ceremonial pottery excavated there suggests that chocolate played an important role in daily life, marking the earliest known use of chocolate by humans.

The hieroglyph for *cacao*, which looks like a fish, has been found on many vessels and bowls, but archaeologists did not know what it meant until the late 1980s, when it was deciphered as *ka-ka-wa*, or *cacao*. The most famous chocolate pot in the world is probably the Rio Azul vessel, which dates to the year 500 and was excavated from a royal Maya burial site in Guatemala in 1984. Not only was it inscribed with the glyph for *cacao*, but it also had chocolate residue preserved inside, beneath a lid that locked into place.

The Princeton vase (named for the museum where it is now located) provides another important piece of evidence about the use of chocolate among the Maya. The vessel dates to about 750 and is decorated with mythological scenes. In one of them, a woman is depicted holding a jar from which she pours a dark substance into a larger jar at her feet. This is believed to be the oldest image of the chocolate beverage in the process of being made, and it explains how the Mesoamericans were able to produce the foam that was considered a very desirable aspect of the drink.

Archaeologists continue to discover evidence that reinforces the importance of cacao in Mesoamerica. In Belize, for example, the tomb of a young aristocrat was found to contain a number of high-status offerings, among them a ceramic vessel. The glyph on the object, translated by David Stuart and Stephen D. Houston (the two scholars who had first deciphered the word *ka-ka-wa*), reads in part: "his drinking vessel for the 'seasoned' cacao."

At a Maya site in Copán, in present-day Honduras, many ceramic containers have been found inscribed with the word *ka-ka-wa,* although none with any chemical evidence of chocolate. Large stone vessels that may have been used as storage or for incense burners have been found with ornate carvings, some with cacao pods and others with cacao trees. According to Stuart, many of the cacao trees carved on the stone vessels are shown as the upraised tail and legs of an alligator, a visual metaphor found elsewhere in Mesoamerican art but whose meaning is unclear. Cacao also seems to have played an important

The Rio Azul vessel, which dates to the year 500, was excavated from a royal Maya burial site in Guatemala in 1984. Not only was it inscribed with the glyph for *ka-ka-wa,* or *cacao,* but it also had chocolate residue preserved inside, beneath a lid that locked into place.

An Aztec vessel used for drinking chocolate

LA PLANTA DEL CACAO

When Diego Rivera began the frescoes in the Palacio Nacional in Mexico City in 1929, his intention was to portray the history of Mexico. Inspired by his country's pre-Columbian past, Rivera rejected the European-derived imagery and style he had been taught in art school and turned to bold colors and simple forms to depict his world. The Aztecs and the Maya had painted events of their lives on the walls of their most important structures, and Rivera and the other Mexican muralists paid homage to this tradition by leaving their public buildings awash with colorful images of Mesoamerican history.

The Palacio Nacional had been built in Mexico City in 1523 over the ruins of the palace of the Aztec ruler Montezuma. One of the many monumental scenes Rivera painted on the walls of the palace is a narrow panel called *La Planta del Cacao* (The Cacao Plant). The fact that Rivera included the story of chocolate along with the legend of Quetzalcoatl and the Mexican Revolution in 1917 reveals his awareness of the importance of chocolate to the people of Mexico.

role in the cosmology, although that too is yet to be clearly understood.

Sculptures, stelae (carved stone monuments or gravestones), wooden lintels, and wall murals on which cacao is depicted have also been discovered and studied. One of the murals at Bonampak, an archaeological site in southern Mexico, shows a royal family with several large white sacks labeled with "five pi ka-ka-wa" placed at the foot of the throne. Stuart has suggested that the word *pi* stands for a unit of eight thousand, indicating that the king was being given forty thousand beans.

At the time the Spanish arrived in what is now Mexico, cacao was being cultivated by Maya farmers in the Yucatán peninsula and traded in a wide network throughout Mesoamerica. The Florentine Codex, for example, illustrates cacao being transported to the Aztec empire. In 1502 Christopher Columbus encountered a Maya trading canoe carrying cacao beans moving north along the Caribbean coast between Costa Rica and Nicaragua, probably on the way to Mexico, "clear evidence," according to historian Allen Young, "of advanced harvesting of cacao beans in Costa Rica by the sixteenth century." Columbus, however, was not interested in those "almonds which in New Spain are used for money," according to another report. He was looking for real gold, which is what drove the Spanish court to sponsor other voyages to the New World.

Although the primary Spanish goal in the New World was to exploit its riches, another was to convert its people to Christianity. In fact, some of the most valuable information we have about pre-Columbian society comes from those who followed

This image from the Florentine Codex, commissioned by the Spanish monk Fray Bernardino de Sahagun, shows offerings of cacao being made to an Aztec god.

OPPOSITE In 1951 Diego Rivera painted *La Planta del Cacao* (The Cacao Plant) in his famous series of murals at the Palacio Nacional in Mexico City.

Traders who walked long distances carrying sacks of valuable cacao seeds were attractive targets for thieves, so they were often accompanied by warriors. This image is from the Florentine Codex.

the conquistadors, the missionaries, who were intent on learning about native culture and beliefs in order to facilitate religious conversion. The journals and reports to Spain of these early ethnographers, like those of the explorers, contain fascinating observations, including a good deal about chocolate.

When Hernán Cortés arrived in the island city of Tenochtitlán, the powerful Aztec empire was ruled by its ninth emperor, Montezuma II. This was an impressive city of towers, temples, bridges, canals, gardens, an aqueduct, and a grand public market. The arrival of Cortés and his Spanish army was not a surprise to the Aztec emperor. Not only had messengers at the coast sent periodic reports of the approaching Spanish vessels, their subsequent landing, and the march inland, but a series of natural events ten years earlier—comets, fires, and floods—had been viewed by Montezuma's seers as omens of impending conflict or crisis. Legend also has it that the appearance of the white, bearded Cortés coincided with the return of the white, bearded Mesoamerican god Quetzalcoatl as predicted in the Aztec calendar.

The Maya god Ek Chuah (or Ekchuah) was the patron of merchants and the protector of cacao growers, but Quetzalcoatl was the deity who had first brought the beans from heaven according to ancient myth. Quetzalcoatl, the plumed serpent, was among the most ancient and powerful deities of the intricate Mesoamerican belief system, integral to nearly every aspect of daily life. He taught the arts, medicine, and agriculture, and as the gardener of paradise, he trained his people how to grow the cacao tree. Quetzalcoatl was a happy

CHOCOLATE: A VERBAL HISTORY

In Nahuatl, the primary indigenous language of Mesoamerica, which is spoken today by more people (1.5 million) than any other Native American language, the word for cacao bean and chocolate is *cacahuatl.* The Spanish did not find Nahuatl easy to understand, and since they had difficulty pronouncing words ending in "tl," they gave many Nahuatl words a "te" ending. It doesn't seem far from *cacahuatl* to *chocolate,* but there are other, equally plausible theories.

Some scholars believe that "chocolate" derives from the Nahuatl word *xocoatl* (*xoco* meaning bitter and *atl* meaning water), and this makes sense, as chocolate made without milk and sugar is most certainly a bitter liquid. Several Maya vessels discovered by archaeologists are inscribed with a hieroglyph that has been deciphered as *ka-ka-wa,* and it seems clear that the Spanish derived the word *cacao* from that word, which obviously related to *cacahuatl.*

Thomas Gage, in his 1648 *New Survey of the West Indies,* presents a view commonly held in Europe at that time that the word *chocolate* was inspired by the sound the water made—choco, choco, choco—when it is stirred in a cup with an instrument called a molinillo, "until it bubble and rise unto a froth." Gage was apparently unaware of the fact that the indigenous word *cacahuatl* existed long before the invention of the molinillo.

Anthropologists Sophie and Michael Coe offer another theory, that words "innocuous in one language often become exceedingly embarrassing when they are transferred into another cultural and linguistic setting." The Coes speculate that the word *caca,* Spanish for excrement, caused the Spanish to change it to a more acceptable term. "It is hard to believe the Spaniards were not thoroughly uncomfortable with a noun beginning with caca to describe a thick, dark-brown drink which they had begun to appreciate."

The Mesoamerican glyph for *ka-ka-wa* from the Rio Azul vessel

OPPOSITE This portrait of Montezuma, who lost his empire at the age of 52, shows him dressed in what the Spanish considered royal Indian attire.

The Aztecs presented offerings of cacao to the ancient god Quetzalcoatl, who is often depicted as a feathered serpent. According to legend, it was Quetzalcoatl's rumored return to Mexico that persuaded Montezuma to welcome Cortés.

and popular god, who refused to condone human sacrifice, and for many reasons he remained a beloved figure even after he was expelled from paradise by the god of the night sky.

When Cortés landed his fleet at what is now Veracruz on Good Friday, April 22, 1519, the Aztecs believed that he was Quetzalcoatl returning from over the sea accompanied by other deities. According to William Prescott, historian of the Mexican conquest: "On the day that Cortés arrived, Montezuma had left his own quarters to welcome him. But the Spanish commander, distrusting, as it would seem, however unreasonably, his good faith, received him so coldly that the Indian monarch withdrew, displeased and dejected." Undaunted, Montezuma eventually accommodated Cortés by building him a house and installing a garden that included, according to one account, "two thousand feet of those trees whose nuts are used for money." (This cannot, of course, have been an accurate observation, as cacao trees cannot grow in dry central Mexico.)

With the help of other native peoples who resented the Aztec ruler and Malinche, the young Indian woman who served as his interpreter, Cortés managed to capture the city of Tenochtitlán and take Montezuma hostage, a

DAY OF THE DEAD

In Mexico, *el Dia de los Muertos* (The Day of the Dead) is observed each year on November 2. Altars are constructed in homes and on grave sites where families welcome the souls of their dead loved ones who return home at this time each year. The altar, or *ofrenda,* contains dishes of food such as tamales and chicken mole. Traditionally there are candles, photos of the deceased, flowers (marigolds), sugar skulls, a glass of water, and always a dish of cacao beans. In Oaxaca at this time of year it is common for family and friends to exchange homemade chocolate.

MOLE

One of the great wonders of the Mexican kitchen, mole is a complex dish that takes hours to prepare. It contains chiles (there are more than twenty varieties to pick from), nuts, spices (peppercorns, cloves, cinnamon sticks), and bundles of herbs (thyme, marjoram, oregano). All of these ingredients are roasted and ground along with cacao beans. To this, families add their own unique ingredients, from apples to plantains, from fire-roasted avocado leaves to raisins. In Oaxaca, this dish is always made for the Day of the Dead, and indeed for any important celebration. One popular legend about the origin of mole is that it was invented by nuns at the Convent of Santa Rosa outside Mexico City when they were inspired by the news of an impending visit from a viceroy to create a special sauce. Chocolate, a revered substance, was certainly one way to make it unique.

Los Santos Reyes (All Kings Day), which is celebrated on January 6 (Epiphany), is another important Mexican holiday. It begins with a symbolic reenactment of the journey of the Three Wise Men carrying gifts of gold, incense, and myrrh to the Christ Child. After the ceremony, foamy hot chocolate is served with a sweet cake (*rosca*) in the form of a ring, which symbolizes a crown. Baked inside the cake is a porcelain doll; the person who finds it is considered lucky.

TOP TO BOTTOM An altar prepared for the Day of the Dead, in Oaxaca; a mole dish; a chocolate *metate*

move that led to the surrender of the capitol on August 13, 1521. With one stroke, Cortés became ruler of a vast area that stretched from the Caribbean to the Pacific Ocean. When political troubles forced him to return to Spain in 1528, he took with him examples of the New World's mineral and agricultural goods, among which were undoubtedly some of the cacao beans treasured by the Aztecs as currency and used to make a special drink favored at Montezuma's court.

Cortés may not have appreciated the royal drink, for it was reported to be extremely bitter, but others did. "When one has drunk this beverage, one can travel all day without fatigue and without taking any nourishment," wrote Bernal Díaz del Castillo, a soldier in Cortés's army whose memoir, published many years after his journey, remains one of the most famous accounts of the conquest. He described in vivid detail the feasts hosted by Montezuma: "From time to time, they brought him, in cup-shaped vessels of pure gold, a certain drink made from cacao, and the women served this drink to him with great reverence." After Montezuma finished dining, his army was fed, along with the house servants: "...it seems to me they brought out over a thousand dishes

An Aztec view of a battle with the Spanish, who were armed with guns, cannons, armor, horses, and enemies of the Aztecs

The conquest of Tenochtitlán, depicted by a sixteenth-century Spanish artist

This rollout photograph of a Maya vessel shows a king being served a chocolate beverage.

of the food of which I have spoken, and then over two thousand jugs of cacao all frothed up, as they make it in Mexico, and a limitless quantity of fruit, so that with his women and female servants and bread makers and cacao makers, his expenses must have been very great." Some observers reported that Montezuma, who is said never to have used anything twice, tossed all those gold goblets into the lake after they were used. However, Bartolomé de las Casas, a Dominican monk sympathetic to the indigenous people of Mexico, noted that the drinking cups were not made out of gold, but were painted gourds.

The chocolate drink served in Montezuma's court and only to the nobility, warriors, or merchants was seasoned with peppers, achiote (from annatto seed), vanilla, and corn. The resulting drink, served cold, was spicy and usually bitter, although some reports indicate that honey was occasionally mixed into the brew. For the most part, the beverage did not appeal to the Spanish palate. As one soldier wrote in his diary, cacao "would be better thrown to the pigs than consumed by men." A recipe recorded in 1631 by Spanish physician Antonio Colmenero reads: "For every hundred cacao beans, mix two pods of chile or Mexican pepper . . . or, failing those, two Indian peppercorns, a handful of aniseeds, two of those flowers known as 'little ears' or vinacaxtlides, and two of those known as mesasuchil.... Instead of the latter, one could include the powder of six roses of Alexandria, a little pod of logwood, two drachmas of cinnamon, a dozen almonds and as many hazelnuts, half a pound of sugar, and enough annatto to give color to the whole."

The Spanish were probably more impressed by the fact that cacao beans were used as money than they were intrigued by its use as a drink. Gonzalo Fernández de Oviedo y Valdés, a historian for the Spanish court between 1532 and 1557, described cacao cultivation practices and also noted that dried cacao beans were used in sixteenth-century Nicaragua as money. He wrote that a rabbit could be purchased at market for ten beans, a horse or a mule for fifty, and a slave for one hundred. Another Spaniard found in an Aztec palace a royal account book that listed as yearly revenue eight thousand turkeys and about one hundred thousand tons of cacao. One conquistador, the brutal Peter de Alvarado, was reported looting Montezuma's royal storehouse of cacao

"O blessed money, which not only gives to the human race a useful and delightful drink, but also prevents its possessors from yielding to infernal avarice, for it cannot be piled up, or hoarded for a long time."

PETER MARTYR D'ANGHIERA

A Spanish engraving, dated c. 1620, showing Mexicans drinking their favorite beverage

This type of incense burner is still used by descendants of the ancient Maya to make offerings of cacao.

beans, which was reputed to contain as many as 960 million seeds, and Cortés himself later participated in collecting cacao tribute from Aztec subjects, because it could be traded for gold when he ran low on funds.

Reports sent to the Spanish court between 1511 and 1530 by Peter Martyr D'Anghiera, an Italian who became a chaplain and historian, wrote about "the particulars concerning the money, but we did not yet know how the tree producing it was planted and cultivated." He considered cacao "doubly useful," as both a beverage and as currency. "The beans are crushed, and a handful of the powder thus obtained is thrown into water and stirred for some time until it produces a truly royal drink." D'Anghiera did not himself travel to the New World, but he carefully compiled his history, published in 1530 as *De Orbe Novo* [About the New World], from reports and interviews with all those who had returned to Spain. He wrote that cacao trees needed a climate that was both warm and damp. "They are planted under the shade of a tree which protects them from the sun's rays or against the dangers of fog, just as a child is sheltered in the bosom of a nurse."

It did not take long for the Spanish missionaries to realize that cacao trees were also considered sacred to the Mesoamericans and that the cacao seeds and the beverage made from them were used in rituals and as offerings to the gods. A Dominican friar named Diego Durán, born in Spain about 1537, was taken to Mexico as a child. The Aztec capital was by then in ruins, but Durán, who understood the Nahuatl language, was able in later years to interview many witnesses of the conquest. He interviewed many natives along with aging Spanish conquerors, and he studied manuscripts, many of which no longer exist. He compiled the results of his research in three important books, *Book of the Gods and Rites, The Ancient Calendar,* and *The History of the Indies of New Spain.*

Durán's manuscripts were lost for nearly three hundred years until they were discovered in the National Library of Madrid in the early 1850s by the Mexican scholar José Fernando Ramírez. The manuscripts were in poor condition, thanks to an inadequate nineteenth-century binding and some apparent censorship (a section about the Spanish soldiers seizing Montezuma's harem had been crossed out), but the illustrations, which had been carefully copied by a priest from original indigenous drawings, were preserved in this remarkable series of documents. Durán's intention had been to understand the native people and their ways in order to convert them; unlike his predecessors, he deplored the burning of the ancient codices, because the clergy could have used them as a means of understanding the Indians.

Durán was especially fascinated by the similarities he saw between personages, rites, and events in the Old Testament and those in Aztec religious life, and he also described how cacao was used in ceremonies and rituals. In the religion of the Aztecs, the primary god, Huitzilopochtli, required more than just food offerings; he demanded human blood, which was considered the most precious food of all. This practice required a steady supply of victims who would willingly give up their lives for the honor of having their hearts given to the god. Durán reports that when the elders appointed a sacrificial victim, they would watch for signs of melancholia and would prepare a special beverage to improve his spirits. The beverage was chocolate, prepared with the bloody water used to wash the sacrificial knives. "It is said that the draught had this effect on him: he became almost unconscious and forgot what he had been told. Then he returned to his usual cheerfulness and dance, having forgotten the warning he had been given." Blood was often sprinkled over ritual offerings of cacao beans, as well as over the beverage and the items of food to be consumed at the ritual feasts, which frequently ended with the drinking of chocolate.

For many Mesoamericans, the cacao pod symbolized the heart and could be used as an offering to the gods. In the 1950s, a study of cacao use among the Maya and Aztecs considered the similarities in shape between the pod and the heart a factor but concluded that the more logical explanation was that both were "repositories of precious liquids—blood and chocolate."

ERRATA

Owing to a printer's error, the text on pages 47, 48, and 49 is repeated on pages 50, 52, and the top of 53, resulting in the omission of the following four paragraphs at the end of the chapter:

In spite of some negative reactions, chocolate received more than its share of high praise from the Baroque age well into the Enlightenment, earning such descriptive names as Mexican nectar, the Indian nut, and manna from Caracas. As chocolate became more widely available, people began experimenting with new ways of using it. Chocolate began to appear in cakes, pastries, and sorbets. In modern-day America, where hot chocolate has become a mass-marketed, marshmallow-laden drink for children, it is difficult to envision the beverage as a delicacy for the top level of European society, a beverage with special powers, as a mid-nineteenth century reference book described it: "This aliment is favourable to idleness, augments the calm of the body and mind, and plunges one in a sweet quietude of *far niente* at a small expense."

A Dutch chemist is largely to thank for helping to bring chocolate-making into a new dimension. In 1828, Coenraad Van Houten patented a process for extracting cacao butter from roasted beans. His screw press reduced the cocoa butter content by nearly half and created a cake that could be pulverized into a fine powder, which we call cocoa. Van Houten's second great invention, based on his knowledge of Mexican history and the fact that Indian doctors had added ash from their fires to cacao, was to treat the highly acidic cocoa powder with alkaline salts such as potash or sodium carbonate. This allowed the cocoa to dissolve more easily in water and made the flavor more mellow and the color lighter. This process, known as "dutching," and the cocoa press are still used by chocolate makers today.

In addition to providing the general populace with a less fatty chocolate beverage, Van Houten's process of reducing the cocoa-butter content also led to the manufacture of chocolate for eating. Chocolate could now be combined with sugar and then blended with the extracted cocoa butter to create solid chocolate. In 1849 the English chocolate maker Joseph S. Fry made what is arguably the world's first eating chocolate, in the form of a bar that he called "Chocolat Délicieux à Manger." Surely his lucky customers would have agreed that chocolate was indeed delicious to eat!

Chocolate made its way to Switzerland relatively late, but it did not take long for Swiss chocolate to attain a position of eminence in Europe, where it contributed significantly to the development of the chocolate industry. The Swiss confectioner Daniel Peter produced the first milk chocolate in 1875, combining a powdered condensed-milk formula devised by chemist Henri Nestlé with cocoa, cocoa butter, and sugar. Another Swiss invention came in 1880 (or 1879) by way of Rodolphe Lindt, who devised a process of grinding cacao nibs into a fine paste with sugar, vanilla, and cocoa butter; he accidently left the grinding machine on all night and the result was a smooth and velvety texture that we now expect when we bite into a chocolate bar. Lindt made some adjustments to the grinder, or conch, and refined the process, which is called conching. Switzerland leads the world in chocolate consumption, nearly twenty-two and a half pounds per person each year, whereas in Spain, chocolate's gateway to Europe, the annual consumption rate is a mere seven and a half.

"The divine drink which builds up resistance
and fights fatigue. A cup of this precious drink
permits a man to walk for a whole day without food."

Hernán Cortés

Chocolate Goes Abroad

Chocolate was introduced to Europe after the conquest of Mexico, but its manufacture remained a secret of the Spanish court for almost one hundred years. Spain also controlled the supply of cacao until the late seventeenth century, by establishing and operating cacao plantations on islands throughout the Caribbean, from Haiti to Trinidad, and in Central and South America. In 1810 Venezuela produced half the world's supply of cacao beans. There was even a Spanish cacao plantation on the island of Fernando Pó (now known as Bioko) off the coast of West Africa. Hernán Cortés and his army had come to the New World in search of gold but stumbled instead on something far more valuable.

It is widely believed that Cortés introduced cacao beans to Spain when he returned in 1528 with many samples of the New World's agricultural and mineral riches—not to mention a few human specimens, including one of Montezuma's sons. Cortés and his men had tasted the cacao beverage in Mexico, and many of the Spanish who remained in the New World developed a taste for chocolate, albeit an altered version. A delegation of Maya from Guatemala was recorded as bringing chocolate to the Spanish court in 1544, when they presented to the prince a number of gifts, including quetzal feathers, corn,

Chocolate in Mexico today reflects the Spanish influence in the addition of sugar and cinnamon, among other flavorings.

OPPOSITE This portrait of Hernán Cortés by Maestro Saldana is in the collection of the National Museum of History, Mexico City.

RIGHT A ceramic mural dated 1710 in the Museum of Ceramics in Barcelona depicts members of the Spanish aristocracy at a reception. The servants are preparing chocolate, which gentlemen are serving to their ladies.

OPPOSITE, ABOVE This illustration from Philippe Dufour's 1685 book, *The Manner of Making Coffee, Tea, and Chocolate,* shows a Turk, a Chinese, and an Aztec with their respective beverages.

ABOVE Molinillos

OPPOSITE, BELOW This still life, painted in 1652 by the Spanish artist Antonio de Pereda y Salgado, shows utensils used in the preparation of chocolate, together with the toasted bread that was dipped into the beverage (today the Spanish prefer churros). At the left is a chocolate pot, with a molinillo beside it; on the saucer is a spoon used to skim the cocoa butter. In the right middle ground are cakes of cocoa powder.

copal, and chocolate. Whether the royal family partook of this last delicacy is not known, but it is likely that they did not, for the "royal drink" of Montezuma would have tasted more like a bitter medicinal brew to the European palate than a delicious beverage.

According to an English physician named Henry Stubbe, who wrote a book called *The Indian Nectar* in 1662, "the Indians, as they are in all things, almost affect a simplicity, so in the making of Chocolata they did not multiply Ingredients; and cared rather to preserve their health, than to indulge their palates, of which they had been so solicitous, that, had not the Spanish luxury and curiosity varied its composition with a multiplicity of mixtures...we had never been acquainted with this drink." Stubbe was only partly correct. Mesoamericans added plenty of other ingredients when they made "Chocolata," but they were just not to European tastes. The Spanish physician Antonio Colmenero wrote of the various indigenous ingredients, including herbs, flowers, and peppers, that were available in Mexico. "In Spain they put in a powder of Roses of Alexandria. I have spoken of all these ingredients, that everyone may make choices of those that please him best, or are most proper for his infirmities," he wrote.

Although chocolate was widely regarded for its medicinal properties (see pages 63–69), some adjustments made by the Spanish to render it more palatable transformed the drink into something far more appealing. The Spanish had imported sugar cane from the Canary Islands and planted it in Mexico, and it was just a matter of time before someone saw the wisdom in adding that ingredient instead of peppers to bitter chocolate. Once the sugar was added, and vanilla, cinnamon, and aniseed won out over chile peppers, achiote, corn-meal, and various native herbs, chocolate became a favorite drink among the Spanish in Mexico and eventually in Spain as well. Some scholars believe that the Aztecs may have added achiote to the chocolate less for its flavor and more for its red coloring—a substitute perhaps for blood, the essential ingredient in so many of their rituals.

The Spanish learned from the Mexicans to heat the chocolate in water, but instead of pouring it from one pot to another, they devised a carved wooden stick called a *molinillo* to dissolve the chocolate and achieve the desired froth. A truly palatable chocolate was perfected in monastery kitchens; some scholars credit Spanish monks with mixing in sugar, and convent nuns with developing chocolate recipes using popular spices. The Spanish made the paste into cakes, as the Maya had done, for easy storage and use. Even today, Mexican chocolate can be purchased in the form of round cakes of crushed cacao nibs combined with sugar, cinnamon, and sometimes almonds.

"In Spain they have very good chocolate, but people are scarcely disposed to send such a distance for it, for all persons are not equally clever in making it; more-over, when they have received from Spain an inferior quality they are obliged to drink it as is. Italian chocolates do not suit the French palate; the bean is generally too much burnt, which gives the chocolate a bitter taste and makes it less nutritious. . . . The use of chocolate has become quite common in France, and everybody thinks they can make it; but very few have arrived at perfection, as the art is far from being an easy one."

ANTHELME BRILLAT-SAVARIN,
La Physiologie du goût (1825)

This porcelain chocolate pot, made c. 1780 in Copenhagen, is similar to the type of pots used for coffee, except that it has a hole in the top of the lid through which a molinet, or molinillo, was used to whisk the beverage in order to preserve the emulsion of cacao butter, flavorings, water, and egg yolks.

In the ceremonies held by the Confrèrerie des Chocolatiers in France, a guild of chocolate makers, the head of the organization wears robes and a headdress with the effigy of Quetzalcoatl, described as the Aztec God of Chocolate, recognizing that no matter how greatly Europeans may have changed chocolate, it remains true to its origins.

OPPOSITE Mlle. de Charolais disguised as a monk with a cup of chocolate nearby, painted by the eighteenth-century French artist Charles Joseph Natoire

Chocolate was introduced to Europe after the conquest of Mexico, but its manufacture remained a secret of the Spanish court for almost one hundred years. Spain also controlled the supply of cacao until the late seventeenth century, by establishing and operating cacao plantations on islands throughout the Caribbean, from Haiti to Trinidad, and in Central and South America. In 1810 Venezuela produced half the world's supply of cacao beans. There was even a Spanish cacao plantation on the island of Fernando Pó (now known as Bioko) off the coast of West Africa. Hernán Cortés and his army had come to the New World in search of gold but stumbled instead on something far more valuable.

It is widely believed that Cortés introduced cacao beans to Spain when he returned in 1528 with many samples of the New World's agricultural and mineral riches—not to mention a few human specimens, including one of Montezuma's sons. Cortés and his men had tasted the cacao beverage in Mexico, and many of the Spanish who remained in the New World developed a taste for chocolate, albeit an altered version. A delegation of Maya from Guatemala was recorded as bringing chocolate to the Spanish court in 1544, when they presented to the prince a number of gifts, including quetzal feathers, corn, copal, and chocolate. Whether the royal family partook of this last delicacy is not known, but it is likely that they did not, for the "royal drink" of Montezuma would have tasted more like a bitter medicinal brew to the European palate than a delicious beverage.

According to an English physician named Henry Stubbe, who wrote a book called *The Indian Nectar* in 1662, "the Indians, as they are in all things, almost affect a simplicity, so in the making of Chocolata they did not multiply Ingredients; and cared rather to preserve their health, than to indulge their palates, of which they had been so solicitous, that, had not the Spanish luxury and curiosity varied its composition with a multiplicity of mixtures...we had never been acquainted with this drink." Stubbe was only partly correct. Mesoamericans added plenty of other ingredients when they made "Chocolata," but they were just not to European tastes. The Spanish physician Antonio Colmenero wrote of the various indigenous ingredients, including herbs, flowers, and peppers, that were available in Mexico. "In Spain they put in a powder of Roses of Alexandria. I have spoken of all these ingredients, that everyone may make choices of those that please him best, or are most proper for his infirmi-

The leisurely taking of morning chocolate did not entirely disappear in the twentieth century. Colette, in her 1946 memoirs, *The Evening Star: Recollections,* looked back on various aspects of her life and realized that "suddenly it was no longer a matter of so many pleasures.... The demi-mondaines stopped getting up late, drinking frothy chocolate in bed while toying with a small dog."

RIGHT Austria's empress, Maria Theresa, and her family at their morning chocolate, c. 1760. The little girl with the doll is the future queen of France, Marie Antoinette. Since the Hapsburgs ruled both Spain and Austria, it is not surprising that chocolate was especially popular at the Viennese court.

OPPOSITE This eighteenth-century French engraving depicts a lady taking her bath while her maid brings in a tray and offers her the choice of a drink of chocolate or a love letter.

ties," he wrote.

Although chocolate was widely regarded for its medicinal properties (see pages 63–69), some adjustments made by the Spanish to render it more palatable transformed the drink into something far more appealing. The Spanish had imported sugar cane from the Canary Islands and planted it in Mexico, and it was just a matter of time before someone saw the wisdom in adding that ingredient instead of peppers to bitter chocolate. Once the sugar was added, and vanilla, cinnamon, and aniseed won out over chile peppers, achiote, cornmeal, and various native herbs, chocolate became a favorite drink among the Spanish in Mexico and eventually in Spain as well. Some scholars believe that the Aztecs may have added achiote to the chocolate less for its flavor and more for its red coloring—a substitute perhaps for blood, the essential ingredient in so many of their rituals.

The Spanish learned from the Mexicans to heat the chocolate in water, but instead of pouring it from one pot to another, they devised a carved wooden stick called a *molinillo* to dissolve the chocolate and achieve the desired froth. A truly palatable chocolate was perfected in monastery kitchens; some scholars credit Spanish monks with mixing in sugar, and convent nuns with developing

The Penthièvre family enjoying their chocolate, by
the eighteenth-century French painter Jean
Baptiste Charpentier

chocolate recipes using popular spices. The Spanish made the paste into cakes, as the Maya had done, for easy storage and use. Even today, Mexican chocolate can be purchased in the form of round cakes of crushed cacao nibs combined with sugar, cinnamon, and sometimes almonds.

It did not take long for chocolate to become all the rage among the elite of Mexico, then Spain, and eventually, the rest of Europe. One famous incident in seventeenth-century Chiapas is often told as an example of how powerful chocolate fever can be. Apparently, a number of Creole women found that they could not make it all the way through Mass without taking their chocolate, which their servants would serve them in church. This behavior enraged the bishop, but the ladies ignored his request to stop, arguing that the long service made them weak and that the chocolate sustained them. When he threatened to excommunicate anyone taking chocolate in church, they responded by boycotting the church, whereupon he threatened to excommunicate anyone who boycotted the church. Shortly thereafter, however, the bishop became ill and died. The rumor was that someone had poisoned his chocolate.

Chocolate has always stirred passion along with debate (even today the European Union has issues over the definition of chocolate), but nowhere more so than among Europeans in the seventeenth century. The two most serious arguments over chocolate at that time were medical and ecclesiastical in nature. No one could agree, for example, about the health benefits of chocolate. Disagreement was particularly heated over whether chocolate could be taken during Lent without breaking a fast. Although much had been made of the beverage's nutritional qualities, it was unclear whether chocolate was a food or a drink. In 1662 Cardinal Francesco Maria Brancaccio declared: "Drinks do not break a fast; wine, though very nourishing, does not break it in the least. The same applies to chocolate, which is undeniably nourishing but is not, for all that, a food."

A number of treatises condemning the use of chocolate were published in the seventeenth century, but no consensus was reached. Although many Jesuits contributed to the development of chocolate, the order of Dominicans opposed "the use, or rather abuse, of certain aromatic plants in the beverage from Mexico known as chocolate." As we all know, religious condemnation can make a forbidden fruit irresistible, and this was certainly true of the fruit of *Theo-*

"Monseigneur was in his inner room, his sanctuary of sanctuaries, the Holiest of Holies to the crowd of worshippers in the suite of rooms without. Monseigneur was about to take his chocolate. Monseigneur could swallow a great many things with ease, and was by some few sullen minds supposed to be rather rapidly swallowing France; but, his morning's chocolate could not so much as get into the throat of Monseigneur without the aid of four strong men besides the Cook.

"Yes. It took four men, all ablaze with gorgeous decoration, and the Chief of them unable to exist with fewer than two gold watches in his pocket, emulative of the noble and chaste fashion set by Monseigneur's lips. One lackey carried the chocolate-pot into the sacred presence; a second milled and frothed the chocolate with the little instrument he bore for that function; a third presented the favored napkin; a fourth (he of the two gold watches) poured the chocolate out."

CHARLES DICKENS,
A Tale of Two Cities (1859)

broma cacao.

The Spanish court and clergy were the first in Europe to use chocolate, but in this period of political marriages and mergers among European royalty and of travel within the monastic world, chocolate soon made its way from Spain to the rest of Europe, although it remained a luxury item for the wealthy as it was heavily taxed. An Italian merchant, Antonio Carletti, is given credit for taking chocolate to Italy in 1606 after having traveled to Central America, where he visited a cacao plantation. He presented his report on this unique substance to Ferdinand I de' Medici, the grand duke of Tuscany, but chocolate did not become widely used until many years later.

Interior of an English chocolate shop

A young man drinking cocoa in an English shop, c. 1890

It's a chocolate, chocolate, chocolate world. And what a palace it was! It had one hundred rooms, and everything was made of either dark or light chocolate! The bricks were chocolate, and the cement holding them together was chocolate, and the windows were chocolate, and the walls and ceilings were made of chocolate, so were the carpets and the pictures and the furniture and the beds; and when you turned on the taps in the bathroom, hot chocolate came pouring out.

ROALD DAHL, *Charlie and the Chocolate Factory* (1964)

In 1615, Anne of Austria, the daughter of Spain's King Philip III, married Louis XIII of France, and so chocolate arrived at the French court. The Spanish infanta María Theresa married Louis XIV in 1660, and a year later the French medical establishment officially approved chocolate as a medicine. The new French queen was a fanatic chocolate drinker and is said to have declared that, "chocolate and the King are my only passions." One of her maids was nick-named "La Molina," after the stick she used to make chocolate for her queen.

The taking of morning chocolate, particularly in bed, became an integral part of aristocratic life in eighteenth-century Europe, a favorite pastime featured in Wolfgang Amadeus Mozart's *Cosí Fan Tutte,* written in 1790. Despina, the

DUCHAMP'S CONFECTIONS

French artist Marcel Duchamp (1887–1968) made several works of art that incorporate the image of a chocolate grinder (*broyeuse de chocolat*), about which he said: "Always there has been a necessity for circles in my life, for, how do you say, rotation. It is a kind of narcissism, this self-sufficiency, a kind of onanism. The machine goes around and by some miraculous process I have always found fascinating, produces chocolate." Duchamp, a friend of Dadaists and Surrealists and known mostly for his readymades, produced few paintings after *Nude Descending a Staircase, No. 2* (1912), which caused an art-world sensation when it was shown at the Armory Show in New York in 1913.

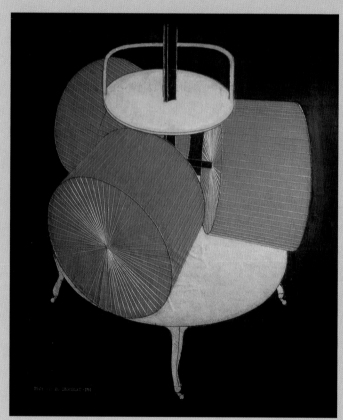

Marcel Duchamp, *Chocolate Grinder, No. 2,* 1914

Duchamp incorporated versions of his two oil paintings *Chocolate Grinder, No. 1* (1913) and *Chocolate Grinder, No. 2* (1914) into his multimedia masterpiece, *The Bride Stripped Bare by Her Bachelors, Even.* This major work, now in the Philadelphia Museum of Art, combines lead foil, wire, mirror silver, dust, oil paint, and varnish applied to glass and mounted between two glass panels that are more than nine feet tall. The piece was begun in 1915 and "finally unfinished" in 1923. In *The Large Glass,* as the work is also known, a chocolate grinder stands in for the male organ in a love affair between eroticized pieces of machinery.

In 1953, Duchamp painted a Minnesota landscape, *Moonlight on the Bay at Basswood,* which is rather traditional save for the materials he used—talcum powder and chocolate. Duchamp worried about the painting, saying that "the poor chocolate, I'm afraid, will disappear or get white."

The artist Man Ray wrote to Duchamp after visiting the French town of Rouen: "You never told me about the Broyeuse de Chocolat. I had to find out for myself.... Would it be an indiscretion on my part to relate that...I was overcome by a most delicious odor of chocolate which grew stronger as I advanced? And then, there they were, in a window, those beautifully polished steel drums churning around in the soft brown yielding mass of exquisite aroma? Later when questioned, you admitted your pure school-boy love."

maid, complains that she must beat her mistress's chocolate for half an hour. But when she sneaks a taste, she finds that her effort has been worthwhile. Taking chocolate in the boudoir was not simply a luxury enjoyed on an idle morning, however, for chocolate was considered by many to be an aphrodisiac. Casanova found it to be a love stimulant along with champagne, and it could, according to one 1702 report, "arouse the ardors of Venus." The drinking of chocolate was a social as well as a sensuous affair. Silver sets and porcelain bowls and cups for serving and drinking chocolate became ever more elaborate. The Spanish even devised a special cup, called a *mancerina,* which nestled in a wide silver or porcelain collar to prevent the imbiber from dribbling on finery.

Chocolate became an even headier brew with the arrival of spices from the East. Ambergris, a waxy substance emitted by sperm whales and found floating in tropical seas, was a favorite flavoring for chocolate, as was *cantharides,* Spanish fly. The marquis de Sade is said to have laced chocolate with those stimulants at a dinner party given by Moreau of Tours. "The marquis had mixed with the dessert a profusion of chocolate, flavored with vanilla, which was found delicious, and of which everybody freely partook. All at once the

A scene from the movie *Chocolat* showing Juliette Binoche with her shop sign

The Oscar-nominated movie *Chocolat,* starring Juliette Binoche, features a mysterious woman who arrives suddenly with her daughter in a small French town and opens a chocolate shop that opens the minds and the hearts of the townspeople. Interestingly, the filmmakers subtly altered the novel by Joanna Harris on which the film is based by introducing elements of Maya culture into the story, spicing the story with the magic of Mexican lore and the true origins of chocolate.

A Rowntree trade card, c. 1925

A Cadbury's chocolate trade card, 1929

Milk chocolate was first produced in Switzerland in 1875, when candy maker Daniel Peter combined cocoa with Henri Nestlé's condensed milk.

guests, both men and women, were seized by a burning sensation of lustful ardour; the cavaliers attacked the ladies without any concealment. The essence of cantharides circulating in their veins left them neither modesty nor reserve in the imperious pleasures." The use of chocolate in connection with aphrodisiacs was not new, however; Montezuma is rumored to have sipped chocolate before visiting his harem.

It became fashionable to lace chocolate with a number of other substances as well, more for novelty than for reasons of altering behavior. The Italian physician and poet Francisco Redi wrote in the mid-1660s: "The court of Tuscany

has found a way of enhancing Spanish perfection with a dash of even more exquisite nobility, thanks to new European ingredients and newly discovered way of adding fresh rinds of citrons and lemons; and the sweet smell of jasmine, mixed with cinnamon, vanilla, amber and musk, makes the chocolate smell quite wonderful to whoever is enjoying it." Redi was keeper of the Medici spicery, and he devised a much sought-after recipe for jasmine chocolate for his patron, Cosimo III de' Medici. The recipe was kept in a safe at the Palazzo Pitti.

London's first chocolate house was established in 1657 by a Frenchman.

A Fry trade card, 1920

Cacao Van Houten, trade card, c. 1900

A newspaper advertisement of the time announced "an excellent West India drink called Chocolate to be sold, where you may have it ready at any time, and also unmade at reasonable rates." The British government imposed a high duty on the import of raw cacao during the seventeenth century, and penalties for smuggling it into the country were severe. However, chocolate houses became very fashionable, as noted by the diarist Samuel Pepys on November 24, 1664: "To a coffee house, to drink jocolatte, very good." At first these establishments attracted members of the upper class looking for social and political discussion, but by the 1800s, as chocolate became less expensive, they became gathering places for working men, a boon to temperance workers, who viewed chocolate as a way of keeping workers away from alcohol.

The chocolate industry in England was largely developed by four Quaker families, Cadbury, Fry, Terry, and Rowntree. As Richard Cadbury wrote in his 1892 book, *Cocoa: All About It:* "It was not until the close of the sixteenth century that Cocoa or Chocolate was generally used in this country, and when we take into account the indifferent means for preparation and the adulterated condition of the article, we can hardly be surprised that it did not come into general favour with the public."

As Cadbury suggests, not everyone in Europe embraced chocolate. "Some people believed that it was a condensed animal jelly whose taste was imparted by various strong-smelling ingredients. Others thought it was a pie containing exotic mushrooms." Much was made of the scum floating on top and the unctuous quality of the beverage, since before the cocoa press was invented in 1828, chocolate could be an oily drink if it was not well mixed, quite different from the drink we know today. One particularly unappetizing report described the chocolate served to British sailors early in the nineteenth century as a drink "as thick as soup, and as greasy as a fish-fryer's thumb. That layer of fat was melted cocoa butter.... Drinking chocolate is better without it: eating chocolate can only be made with it." A neat, Jack-Spratt situation which, when it was finally grasped, led to the discovery of chocolate as we know it. Although tradition has it that rum was what fueled the British fleet, it is a fact that in 1823 British seamen received a ration of one ounce of cocoa every day; in fact, more than half of the cocoa imported into nineteenth-century England was consumed by the Royal Navy.

Take Two M&Ms and Call Me
in the Morning: A Medical History

"Chocolate is most excellent, in nourishing and
preserving health entire, purging by expectoration's,
and especially by the sweat-vents of the body,
preventing unnatural fumes ascending to the head."

William Hughes, *The American Physician*...(1672)

For Mesoamericans, the taking of chocolate was by and large a ritual experience, but for Europeans, chocolate served medicinal rather than spiritual purposes. Medical practices in the sixteenth century were still based on the ancient Greek system in which good health was achieved through a balance of the four humors, or bodily fluids (blood, phlegm, black bile, and yellow bile), which related to the four elements (air, water, earth, and fire), the four qualities (cold, wet, dry, and hot), and the four temperaments (sanguinity, sluggishness, melancholia, and choler). A deficiency or excess of any of the humors would cause pain, but balance could be restored by applying the opposite humor or combination of humors through diet, exercise, and other therapies. Like the humors, foods—alone or in combination—had properties that were either cold or warm, moist or dry, qualities relating not so much to the food's consistency or temperature as to its value as energy. Chocolate, established as a cold, dry food by the experts, would thus be useful in treating fever.

Mesoamericans too had developed medical systems that included a complex blend of ideas involving geographical direction, colors, and religious beliefs, and chocolate played a part as well. As a beverage, it was used to treat stomach complaints, and when combined with liquid extracted from the bark of the kapok tree, it was thought to cure infections as well. Different herbs were blended with cacao to cure infections and diarrhea, and to relieve fever and faintness. One mixture called for an infusion of opossum tail to alleviate cough and phlegm. After the conquest, the Spanish incorporated into their medical training not only some of these ideas but also the ways in which plants of the New World were used as medications.

As we have seen, European conquerors, explorers, and priests were all fascinated by the beverage made from cacao beans, especially by its health-giving attributes, about which many theories were developed. According to various reports, some of them appearing as late as the early twentieth century, chocolate proved to be an effective treatment for a wide array of complaints, including anemia, asthma, cancer, jaundice, and women's ills. Here are a few excerpts:

1500s A book written by a Maya priest (discovered in the Yucatán in 1914 and now at Princeton University), which contains chants and incantations to be spoken over patients suffering from various diseases, prescribed, for skin eruptions, a bowl of medicinal chocolate containing two peppers, honey, and tobacco juice. This potion was also deemed useful for those suffering from fever and seizures.

1529 Bernardino de Sahagun, a Spanish priest, arrived in Mexico, where he compiled oral histories of native informants in a text now called the Florentine Codex. He described various medicinal uses for cacao and included a warning against green cacao, which "makes one drunk, takes effect on one, makes one dizzy, confuses one, makes one sick, deranges one. When an ordinary amount is drunk, it gladdens one, Thus it is said: 'I take cacao. I wet my lips. I refresh myself.'"

1552 The first published illustration of a cacao tree appeared in the Badianus Manuscript, also known as "An Aztec Herbal," compiled at the College of Santa Cruz at Tlaltelco in Mexico City by two Aztec authors, Martín de la Cruz and Juannes Badianus. Among the many remedies cited is a poultice for injured feet that involved mixing a variety of herbs with cacao flowers.

1577 In a botanical study of the plants of "New Spain," Francisco Hernández provided the first detailed description of the cacao tree and all its varieties. He also mentioned numerous nutritional and medical virtues of the "very agreeable beverage" of chocolate. A straight dose of cacao, he writes, is useful for problems of the liver.

1592 Agustin Farfan's *Tratado Breve de Medicina* [Brief Treatise on Medicine] listed the herbs of Mexico and their medicinal uses, noting that chocolate served as a hot beverage is used as a laxative.

1651 An English translation was published of the Spanish physician Antonio Colmenero's tract on chocolate, including this poetic preface: "To every Individuall (sic) Man, and Woman, Learn'd, or unlearn'd, / Honest, or Dishonest: In the due Praise of Divine Chocolate. / Doctors, lay by your irksome books...leave quacking; and enucleate the vertues of our chocolate. / Let the Universall Medicine /(Made up of Dead-mens Bones and Skin,) /Be henceforth Illegitimate, /And Yield to Soveraigne-Chocolate."

A Bibliography of the Nutritive Value of Chocolate and Cocoa

With Quotations and Summaries
Prepared for the Hershey Chocolate Company
by The American Food Journal
Institute

Compliments of the Hershey Chocolate Company
Hershey, Pa., U.S.A.

The preface went on in this vein for twenty more stanzas before Dr. Colmenero had his say. The purpose of his book is to address the "drinke Chocolate," which was very much in use in Spain, Italy, and "Flanders," and to address rumors about the "benefit or hurt they receive from it." It was believed that chocolate was fattening but also that it "strengthens the stomach." Colmenero's first point was to establish the properties of chocolate as cold and dry and its effects on the humors. He added, however, that chocolate "vehemently incites to Venus, and causeth conception in women."

1658 Thomas Gage, the English explorer, cited Colmenero's work and reports other uses of chocolate for medicinal purposes, such as adding cinnamon to promote urine flow or achiote (annatto seed) to alleviate shortness of breath.

1650s The Italian Francisco Redi, chief physician for the Medici household, was also in charge of the apothecary. He created a recipe for jasmine chocolate that Cosimo, the hypochondriac prince, depended upon, although for what exactly isn't clear. Perhaps it cheered him up to think that no one else could delight in the taste—the recipe was a state secret.

1662 In *The Indian Nectar, or a Discourse Concerning Chocolata,* the English explorer Henry Stubbe gave his preferred recipe for Chocolata Royal (mostly for pleasure) made with anise seeds, nutmeg, and cornmeal. Stubbe solicited his readers for anecdotes and other "preparations that I may not be ignorant of what effects Chocolata, or its particular ingredients have here in England...to inform or otherwise benefit men." He also noted that cacao can provoke "lustful desires" and that the addition of vanilla will strengthen the heart. He also notes the high fat content of cocoa and devotes much of his treatise to his experiments in attempting to remove the "oyl." (It would take another 166 years for a Swiss chocolatier to accomplish that feat.)

1672 William Hughes devoted a chapter to the virtues of the chocolate drink in his tract entitled *The American Physician, or a Treatise of the Roots, Plants, Trees, Shrubs, Fruit, Herbs Growing in the English Plantations in America.* He described chocolate as a nourishing and "speedy refreshment after travel, hard labor, or violent exercises." Following his lead, American cookbooks would continue to recommend chocolate as a nutritious breakfast beverage throughout the nineteenth century.

1719 In his *Natural History of Chocolate,* the Frenchman D. de Quelus recommended drinking chocolate for "exhausted spirits" and stated that an ounce of chocolate "contains as much nourishment as a pound of beef." He also warned against its use by sedentary or "fat" people. Quelus also provided recipes that broaden the applications of chocolate, such as mixing it with other substances, including powdered cinnamon for "a good purge."

1727 Sir Hans Sloane, physician to Queen Anne and King George II, combined milk and chocolate to increase the digestibility of chocolate. (Cadbury would use this recipe from 1849 to 1885). It was considered a health food and advertised for its "lightness on the stomach and its great use in all Consumptive cases."

1728: An Italian writer observed: "There is no counting the money that Europeans nowadays spend on cocoa and other chocolate drugs."

1741 Linnaeus, who gave chocolate its botanical name, also examined the medicinal uses of chocolate. In his opinion, three types of illness responded well to chocolate: wasting or thinness brought on by lung and muscle diseases, hypochondria, and hemorrhoids. Linnaeus also mentioned cacao as an effective aphrodisiac.

1825 Anthelme Brillat-Savarin (1755–1826), a French lawyer and author of *La Physiologie du goût* (The Physiology of Taste), published in 1825, offered a recipe for the perfect cure for hangovers, insomnia, and problems with concentration (what we now know as SAD, or seasonal affective disorder). As he put it, "every man of intelligence who feels his faculties temporarily dulled; every one who finds the air damp, time hanging heavily on his hands, and the weather unendurable; every man who is tormented by a fixed idea which deprives him of the liberty of thinking." For these complaints, it was suggested that a pint of chocolate be mixed with between 60 and 72 grains of amber (meaning ambergris).

1846 A. Saint-Arroman wrote of chocolate in his *Coffee, Tea and Chocolate: Their Influence upon the Health, the Intellect and the moral Nature of Man:* "This alimentary paste, which some persons in good health honour with their partiality, and which the physicians recommend to certain sick persons, deserves to be well known, that all may know what temperaments it suits, and in what circumstances it may be injurious." He also warned against adulterations, rampant at the time, by "greedy merchants" extending chocolate with rice flour and other starches. "Strong stomachs always bear it, but there are some that do not digest it without difficulty. Thence proceeds the custom of drinking a glass of water after it.... The ferruginous chocolate, so beneficial to women who are out of order, or have the green sickness [anemia], is prepared by adding the paste of chocolate iron in the state of filings, oxide, or carbonate."

1870 Florence Nightingale, the mother of nursing, considered chocolate a basic staple. A portable kitchen for overworked nurses that included fuel, pots and

for sleep...and energy

CADBURYS
Bourn-vita

More people than ever are enjoying
Bourn-vita. This nightcap is the very best value
for money at 1/10½ *a half pound*

pans, soup, wine, and chocolate could certainly "have saved hundreds of lives," she wrote in her notes.

1895–1930s Chocolate-covered pills were produced by all the major pharmaceutical companies to disguise the bad taste of medicine. (Chocolate Ex-Lax continues to be popular even today.) Interestingly, many chocolate companies had their roots in the pharmacy. Joseph Terry of York, England, started as an apothecary specializing in blood-letting in 1767, but he switched focus to chocolate-making in 1786. Swiss chocolate maker Philippe Suchard became fascinated with chocolate when, as a twelve-year-old, he was sent to the local apothecary for a tonic preparation of chocolate for his sick mother. The fact that the medicine cost the same as a worker's wages for three days perhaps provided an inspiration for this future chocolatier. Many chocolate makers tried to capitalize on the health-related fascination with chocolate. Rowntree, for instance, offered a product in its early days called Homeopathic Cocoa.

1983 Dr. Andrew Weil, author of *From Chocolate to Morphine,* determined that chocolate is a drug. As director of the Integrative Medicine program at the University of Arizona in Tucson, Dr. Weil has written many books on natural medicine and healing. He claims that chocolate contains only a small amount of caffeine "but has a lot of theobromine, a close relative with similar effects." While most people consider chocolate a mere flavor, it is also, according to Weil, "a mood-altering substance that can have strong effects on body and mind and can certainly be addictive."

1994 In his book *The Chocolate Tree,* Allen M. Young wrote: "Chocolate contains more than 300 identified chemical substances, including theobromine and methylxanthine—two mildly addictive caffeine-like substances—and phenylethylamine, a stimulant chemically similar to the human body's own dopamine and adrenaline. Phenylethylamine acts on the brain's 'mood centers' and presumably induces the emotion of falling in love, a matter of only partly understood brain chemistry."

The most recent edition of "Chocolate and Health," a promotional pamphlet published by the Chocolate Manufacturers' Association stated in the introduction: "Despite research to the contrary, chocolate consumption is sometimes associated with deleterious effects on health." The pamphlet contains sections on acne, allergies, and cravings ("women who crave chocolate are likely do so because of its flavor and mouth feel, not because there are 'addictive' substances in chocolate"). Also included is a description of the widely reported latest discovery in chocolate (several studies funded by M&M/Mars), that some chocolates are rich in flavonoid antioxidants, which may be useful in helping to fight cardiovascular disease.

These recent scientific findings are just as welcome today as reports in the past have been to centuries of chocolate lovers. Surely there is truth to be found in these early reports. Take this mid-nineteenth-century passage written by German chemist Baron von Liebig and quoted by the American Walter Baker & Company, which like other chocolate manufacturers occasionally published pamphlets containing recipes and testimonials from nutrition experts. Liebig wrote: "Chocolate is a perfect food.... It agrees with dry temperaments and convalescents; with mothers who nurse their children; with those whose occupations oblige them to undergo severe mental strains; with public speakers, and with all those who give to work a portion of the time needed for sleep. It soothes both stomach and brain, and for this reason, as well as for others, it is the best friend of those engaged in literary pursuits."

"The cacao lands, a region embracing all of the southern part of the
state of Bahia in Brazil, were fertilized by blood."

Jorge Amado, Foreword to *The Violent Land* (1945)

Blood, Sweat, and Chocolate

The Cacao Trade

Not surprisingly, Spain was the first country to control the cacao trade between
Europe and the New World and to establish cacao plantations in the Caribbean and South America. At first, Dutch and English pirates in search of cacao
confined themselves to raiding Spanish ships, but by the 1620s the Dutch had
seized several islands north of the Gulf of Venezuela, including Curaçao, and
Spain began to lose its monopoly. Curaçao became a slave depot as part of
the infamous triangular trade system, in which human cargo from Africa was
traded to plantation owners in the New World for products that were then
loaded on ships bound for Europe. The Atlantic slave trade, which began with
the Portuguese in the fifteenth century, did not legally end in the United States
until 1808 and elsewhere in the Americas until the 1870s.

Spain managed to keep control of most of its cacao-producing territories—
which in later years would be hit by serious plant diseases—but other European countries also joined the rush to provide chocolate for an increasingly
enthusiastic market abroad. About 1660 the French began cultivating cacao on

Harvesting cacao pods in Ghana

their Caribbean possessions Martinique and St. Lucia and eventually expanded into Brazil. The Dutch helped expand the cacao industry into Indonesia as early as 1560; in 1778, the Dutch Batavian Society of Arts and Sciences offered a silver medal "to the first person to plant fifty cacao trees successfully."

At first, the Spanish used local workers to harvest cacao in Mexico and Guatemala, and later in Ecuador and Venezuela. But by the end of the seventeenth century, the native population had declined drastically from a combination of disease and harsh living conditions. West Africa provided Spanish growers with a new source of agricultural labor, and eventually the French, English, and Portuguese also used African slaves to expand cocoa production in their American colonies. The Dutch brought in as many as one hundred thousand slaves a year through their colony in Curaçao. Brazil would not emancipate slaves until after 1880.

The first Spanish slave ships to come from Africa to the Western Hemisphere traded in the West Indies as early as 1532, and the Portuguese brought slaves to Brazil about twenty-five years later to work first on sugar plantations

Slave ship

A West Indies cocoa plantation, c. 1850

and then on other crops. Not all efforts to grow cacao in the European colonies were successful. In 1690, an Englishman, Dalby Thomas, described the early days of British cacao production on the island of Jamaica, where plantations and slaves had been left behind by the Spanish. In his *Historical Account of the Rise and Growth of the West India Collonies, and of the Great Advantages They are to England, In Respect to Trade,* Thomas wrote: "When we conquered, it produced such prodigious profit with little trouble that...several others set up their rests to grow wealthy therein." The new owners planted a great deal of cacao, but "the Spanish slaves had always foretold it would never thrive," and they were right. For about six years, British plantation owners reaped the profits until the crop withered and died "by some unaccountable cause, though they imputed it to a black worm, or grub, which they found clinging to the

Plantation owners in Samoa

roots." The Jamaican cacao groves were eventually wiped out by the unknown plant disease or weather event, which was called the "blast," but for several years the island was England's main source of chocolate. Jamaica still has cacao farms, but the output is relatively small.

A rather different tale was told 150 years later, when a writer living in Trinidad's capital, Port-of-Spain, filed a story in 1845 for a Boston-based magazine in which he described an excursion to a Spanish-owned cacao plantation twenty miles inland. The trip began with a "smart and delightful ride of

The cocoa harvest in Yaou village, Ivory Coast

A cocoa farm in Ghana

nearly two hours along an excellent road, having handsome sugar-plantations on both sides.... I shall not stop here to describe the grandeur of the Arauca forests; suffice it to state, that they are composed of nature's choicest selection of tree and shrub, among which a variety of animals roam, and numerous birds of varied hue and plumage, worthy of such a dwelling, abide and disport."

Eventually he reached the plantation which burst "suddenly and brightly upon one's view...a vast forest-orchard, if I may make use of the term, planted in the space formed by a hollow V between two mountains." The plantation, Reconocimiento, was one of the largest cacao establishments in Trinidad, nearly a mile in length with about thirty thousand cacao trees. "It employed, as far as I recollect, forty effective slaves."

Once there, the reporter was fed a big meal. "I need not say that the beverage of the gods was there—theobroma, chocolate of excellent flavor—and left us nothing to desire." The rest of the visit consisted of hunting, fishing, bathing and "ranging through the delightful groves of the plantation, and occasionally lending a hand to the laborers, in helping them to pick the cacao fruit from the trees."

"The profits of a cacao estate at Trinidad may be imagined to have been very great about the year 1816, a great many years before the time of my visit, when it is considered that the produce was then selling for as much as 25 dollars the fanega [a unit of measure], more than double the price today.... In conclusion, we recommend the Trinidadians and other West Indians who have investments in plantations of it, to stick to their cacao, for it is an easy, light, and gentlemanly culture and occupation, which a man could enact in pumps and silk stockings, and that without spoiling his complexion; although its price be not too encouraging; it is not one third of what it was in 1816."

The Cacao Plantation

Thanks no doubt to such alluring descriptions of life on the cacao plantation, it was not long before cacao had started making its way to the other side of the globe. A memoir entitled *Every Day Life on a Ceylon Cocoa Estate* was published in 1905 by Mary Steuart, who wrote as "a woman to women—the

Workers on a Congo plantation splitting cacao pods

Two women on an Indonesian cacao farm removing cacao seeds from the pods

mothers, sisters, and future wives in England of the young planters of Ceylon." Steuart went to Ceylon to visit her son, who had been transferred off an established estate with its "well-appointed English house" to the more isolated estate of an absent proprietor, where "day after day passes without a glimpse of a white face." In addition to the cacao crop, there is also coffee, pepper, vanilla, rubber, and coconuts. She writes that Ceylon suffered a "great coffee disaster" and thus coffee was replaced by cacao, which had been first brought to Ceylon as an ornamental shrub fifty years earlier. "The picking is a very pretty sight, many women are employed, and their gay clothes and glittering jewelry, and the heaped up red pods give a rich note of colour to the shaded groves in which they work."

But not all was well on the plantation, where some problems caused by ants and fungus were beginning to arise. Also, the new abundance of cocoa had caused prices to decline. "The kindly impulse of our Queen to send a Christmas gift of chocolate to her soldiers in the field proved a perfect godsend to Ceylon cocoa planters. The price immediately rose to nearly its old level... but fell again somewhat when that demand was over." And there were local problems. The straying buffalo belonging to neighboring villages "do infinite damage to the cocoa, knocking down the pods, trampling them underfoot and breaking off the branches. The other enemies are wild pigs who eat the cocoa and dig up quite large holes in the ground whilst hunting for rubber roots, which attract them by their sweetness." Fines were imposed, but the plantation manager was obliged to seize the offending animals and hold them hostage until the money was paid.

It was not easy to keep a plantation going, in spite of ingenious growing ideas. Mrs. Steuart tells us that her son's plantation had attempted to increase the profitability of its crops by using rubber trees as shade for cocoa. Unfortunately, "it was found to be rather injurious than otherwise, for during the hottest time of the year, when cocoa requires shade the most, the rubber trees are bare, and in monsoon time the foliage is so dense that it gives the undergrowth no chance of getting the sunshine that there is." Ceylon still grows cacao but its contribution to overall world production is negligible.

As much as 70 percent of the world's cacao crop today is grown in West Africa, which once provided slaves to harvest cacao in the New World. The Ivory Coast now leads the continent in producing cacao (and in fact is the world's largest supplier of cacao), but Ghana from about 1910 to 1970 produced more cacao beans than any other region. Low prices and other conditions caused many small farmers to change crops during the 1970s, but the story of Ghana's role in the chocolate business had a promising beginning.

In 1878, a Ghanaian named Tete Quarshie smuggled cacao seedlings into his country from Fernando Pó, an island off Equatorial Guinea. He worked there on a farm, and his efforts to grow cacao at home were the subject of a play written by Dei Anang in 1946, entitled *Cocoa Comes to Mampong: Brief Dramatic Sketches Based on the Story of Cacao in the Gold Coast.* In the play, Quarshie searches for the right soil in his homeland and is full of enthusiasm. "Here in this load, I bear the seeds of a wonderful tree which, if cultivated in this land, will bless its sons everlastingly with wealth, and people far and near with health. These are the seeds of the cacao tree which I have brought with me from across the sea."

The plot of land Quarshie chooses is known as Guamanso, which means marketplace, "for to this spot all the famous traders of our land used to bring their wares for sale." Rum is poured on the ground, a libation for the gods, with prayers that the land will be blessed and from "this little patch of land a great industry may rise." And so it did.

The Chocolate Factory

In spite of progress that has been made in the various methods by which chocolate is made, nothing much has changed when it comes to the way cacao is harvested. Workers still use machetes to cut the mature pods from the trees, grueling physical work that takes place twice a year under poor conditions with little pay. In the factory, however, some manufacturers seem to have been more concerned with the welfare of their workers. In America, Milton Hershey proved that a paternalistic factory town with benefits for its residents could be successful, and Cadbury's in England was founded on the basis of high ideals and Quaker principles.

Bournville, the village surrounding the Cadbury factory, was created in 1893 on 123 acres and provided a stocked trout stream for anglers, gardens, a

lawn-tennis court, and sixteen villa residences for workmen who showed "gentle demeanor, diligence in business, and assiduity." In Cadbury's version of compassionate conservatism, workers labored under excellent conditions, although they had to sit still for periodic readings from the Bible. The idea was to create a factory that, as one Cadbury publication put it, "banishes the thought of smoke and machinery" and gives instead a "happy and busy scene of labour." At the entrance to Bournville, one would pass through a garden and experience the "breath of flowers and the song of birds." Another scene the company was very proud of was the sight of "the girls in their white costumes, after dinner, sitting to read under the trees, or enjoying in other ways a breath of fresh air."

Bournville still exists and, like Hershey, created a tourist attraction in its company town. The English chocolate company would rather view Cadbury World as a visitors' center than as a theme park, but it does operate a "gentle ride through a chocolate wonder land!"

The idyllic conditions under which the Cadbury and Hershey employees lived and worked were dramatically different from the terrible conditions to which field workers, many of them slaves even as late as 1910, were subjected. The momentum for change was led by many of the Quaker families that had entered the chocolate business. J. S. Fry & Sons, for instance, found a way to make their disapproval of slavery known early on by boycotting the products of the Portuguese plantations in West Africa. But the struggle against slave labor was a long, ongoing battle.

In 1901, Joseph Burtt, representing an antislavery society in England, was sent on behalf of William Cadbury to the Portuguese-owned African islands of São Tomé and Príncipe (St. Thomas and Princes Islands), as well as West Africa, to investigate the labor situation. Cadbury had been very distressed to learn that some of the cocoa used in his mills in Birmingham was produced by slaves, a realization brought on by crusading journalists who saw an opportunity to expose a possible hypocrisy. The firms of Cadbury, Rowntree, and Stollwercks announced that they would buy no more goods produced by slave labor. Burtt reported, however, that "the Portuguese boasted in their papers... that America would take slave cocoa if England was too squeamish to buy slave labor."

OPPOSITE Some of the 4,300 women employed by Cadbury working at the factory in Bournville, 1954

In 1910 Burtt testified at a special hearing before the U. S. Congressional Committee on Ways and Means that he had found 35,000 to 40,000 Angolan slaves on various plantations and had seen shackles and corpses along the Angolan slave route. "These people regard these islands as death," he reported, "and I know of a case of a woman who had a servant who said that he would like to go to the funeral of his uncle. She said, 'Is your uncle dead?' He answered, 'No; but he has gone to San Thome.' They regard that as the same thing as death."

The questioning of the committee members was long and at times incredulous. Why, went the refrain, didn't the "chaps" just grab a gun or run away? Here is a brief excerpt:

THE CHAIRMAN: Do they try?

MR. BURTT: No. They would not be so foolish.

THE CHAIRMAN: What would happen to them?

MR. BURTT: How would one of your slaves in olden times—

THE CHAIRMAN: No. What would happen to them? I never had any slaves. What would happen?

MR. BURTT: I could not tell you. It is too wild a conjecture.

THE CHAIRMAN: They might be treated like gentlemen for aught you know?

MR. BURTT: They might. Here is a photo a friend of mine took recently. There is a slave lying dead and there is his shackle. That is on the slave route....

The hearing lasted one hour and had the following outcome: "Resolved by the Senate and the House of Representatives of the United States of America and Congress assembled, That the President be, and hereby is, authorized to forbid by proclamation the entry of cocoa into the United States or her possessions when it is shown to his satisfaction that the same is the product of slave labor."

That same year, 1910, Walter Baker & Company in America and England's Cadbury, two of the largest chocolate firms in the world, declared their refusal to use cacao from slave plantations. Other large chocolate companies from that time, including Whitman and Wilbur in the United States, also agreed to stop using cacao harvested by slave labor.

This would be a nice note on which to end the subject of slavery, but unfortunately, the following report appeared in the English newspaper *The Express* as recently as September 27, 2000: "Chocolate, it seems, carries modern-day slavery into our homes." Documentary filmmakers Kate Blewett and Brian Woods had encountered slave conditions on cacao plantations in the Ivory Coast and produced a documentary called *Slavery*. Blewett and Woods had been honored in 1998 with a Robert F. Kennedy Journalism Award for their film *Innocents Lost*, about children stolen from their homes in Bangladesh and elsewhere and taken to the United Arab Emirates to be used as camel jockeys. In preparing a new film about stolen Indian children, some of which were made to work as domestic servants in London and Washington D.C., the filmmakers visited about one hundred small cacao farms in the Ivory Coast, where they also found children being exploited. "We wanted a way of bringing it home to people in the West and not letting it be something people could watch and go 'Isn't it terrible what people in far-off lands do to other people in far-off lands,'" Woods was quoted as saying in an article published in *The Guardian* on September 28, 2000.

In response to the film, the Biscuit, Cake, Chocolate and Confectionery Alliance, speaking on behalf of British chocolate companies, denied any knowledge of slavery but made it clear that its members deplored "slavery and every other form of discrimination and exploitation, and supports all efforts towards eradication."

In the summer of 2001, leading American chocolate manufacturers, through the Chocolate Manufacturers' Association (CMA), launched an initiative to address the issue of workers' rights that were identified by the government of the Ivory Coast. As a result of an investigation prompted by a British television report, the Ivorian government announced that it had uncovered clandestine child trafficking that originated in neighboring countries. "As an industry, we strongly condemn abusive labor practices, and our goal is to be part of the worldwide effort to solve this problem," said Larry Graham, president of the CMA. "If one child is affected, that is one child too many."

War and Chocolate

"What use are cartridges in battle?
I always carry chocolate instead."

George Bernard Shaw, *Arms and the Man* (1894)

In 1908 Oscar Straus adapted his operetta *The Chocolate Soldier* from a play by George Bernard Shaw. Straus took Shaw's pacifist theme and transformed it into light entertainment in which a Swiss mercenary in the Serbian army takes refuge from his Bulgarian enemies in the house of a Bulgarian general. He hides in the daughter's bedroom, where he stuffs himself to distraction on the daughter's stash of chocolates and falls asleep on her bed. When he (known henceforth as the Chocolate Cream Soldier) is discovered, mayhem and romance follow. Shaw was not pleased.

Shaw notwithstanding, chocolate has often played a role in wartime. Beginning with the Aztec warriors, chocolate has been used to boost the energy and morale of soldiers. More than half of the cocoa imported into England in the nineteenth century was consumed by the Royal Navy. British seamen in 1823 received a ration of one ounce of cocoa every day, because it was considered the ideal drink for sailors on watch duty, being nutritious, hot, and non-alcoholic.

It was World War I that really brought chocolate candy into the big time. American chocolate makers were commissioned to produce large blocks of chocolate, which were chopped up and distributed to soldiers abroad. The soldiers

Women packing parcels of tobacco, chocolates, and toiletries to be sent to the troops in World War II.

(who were called doughboys) returned home at the end of the war with a taste for chocolate, and that demand inspired a boom in the candy-bar business. A poster for an American aid organization in 1914, in an effort to boost troop morale, implored citizens to "Send 'em a smoke, send 'em a sweet. Your boy needs tobacco, chocolate, jam...." Robert Whymper, a British chocolate industry expert, wrote in 1921 that "Without tobacco, rum, and chocolate, placed in the order of their necessity, an army in modern warfare would be defeated even with a sufficiency of guns and ammunition."

After the end of World War I, manufacturers could turn their attention away from the making of shells and other munitions to more appealing products. One English company, Joseph Baker, Sons and Perkins, Ltd., after doing its part for the war, began to "boast of providing machinery...for use by the manufacturers of cocoa, chocolate, and confectionery."

A British canteen brings chocolate, tea, and other goods to servicemen stationed in the North Atlantic desert during World War II.

By World War II, the U. S. government recognized the importance of chocolate to the armed forces and allocated valuable shipping space for importing cacao beans into the United States. Many soldiers relied on pocket chocolate bars for strength when food rations dwindled. Today, the U. S. Army D-ration consists of three four-ounce chocolate bars, made without cocoa butter to prevent spoilage. For troops in the Gulf War, Hershey produced a heat-resistant Desert Bar. In her recent book *The Emperors of Chocolate: Inside the Secret World of Hershey and Mars,* author Joël Glenn Brenner describes the corporate battles that took place between the chocolate giants over market share in the Gulf War.

Hershey's Kisses, introduced in 1907, were not made during World War II because of silver-foil rationing and because the equipment had to be freed up for making the military ration chocolate bar. Hershey produced more than 3 billion ration bars between 1942 and 1949. In England, Cadbury supplied ration bars wrapped in brown paper to the Australian armed forces from 1939 to 1945.

The war years put an end to luxuries for civilians at home and abroad; even common household items became hard to get, both in America and abroad. In one of her volumes of memoirs, *The Blue Lantern,* the French writer Colette described visiting Geneva in 1946 after living through six years of blackouts and shortages in Paris. "What! Chocolate for the asking, and gateaux in patisseries still abundantly overflowing when all had eaten their fill!"

> "The superiority of chocolate both for health and nourishment will soon give it the same preference over tea and coffee in America which it has in Spain."
>
> Thomas Jefferson in a letter to John Adams (1785)

Back to America

Our third president was undoubtedly a chocolate lover. We know this from his correspondence and from the detailed account books he kept. For instance, during Thomas Jefferson's stay in Paris, his itemized notes in the hotel bill included the fact that he drank hot chocolate instead of coffee for breakfast. In his household collection at Monticello, his Virginia estate, there is a piece of silver referred to as the family chocolate pot.

But chocolate manufacturing and consumption in North America was still in its nascent years during Jefferson's lifetime. With his taste for chocolate, as with his many other passions, Jefferson was ahead of his time. A mill had opened twenty years earlier, in 1765, along the Neponset River near Dorchester, Massachusetts, an operation that would eventually become Walter Baker & Company (which is still in existence, since 1927 under the umbrella of the food giant General Foods). Baker's head start in providing the United States with chocolate, however, would slow down considerably with the outbreak of the American Revolution in 1775.

At the time of the revolution, most cacao was being grown in the West Indies. Spain had held the monopoly on cacao production since the conquest,

The North American taste in chocolate drinks is a far cry from Montezuma's.

OPPOSITE The famous "Baker's girl" image used as a logo by Baker's, America's oldest chocolate manufacturer, was originally a Viennese chambermaid, immortalized in 1743 by the French painter Jean-Etienne Liotard.

although England and France had seized most of the islands well before the American Revolution and had begun to grow cacao in their own tropical possessions. Cacao shipments to North America were subject to a very high tariff or would have to sneak past the Royal Navy warships patrolling the coast.

It is not surprising, then, that chocolate was little used in the colonies. During the 1760s, one colonial merchant placed advertisements in Virginia newspapers listing items available in his Williamsburg and Richmond stores. His schooner traveled the James River regularly carrying peas, pork, lard, and butter to Philadelphia and returning with items such as earthenware, flour, bread, coffee, iron skillets, saddle trees, soap, furniture, and chocolate.

Account books from 1751 and 1752 in the Williamsburg Foundation archive contain lists of goods purchased from Great Britain by various colonial merchants. Tobacco went to England, and sugar, molasses, chocolate, cheese, tea, beer, raisins, hats, hosiery, and snuff were among the goods that came back.

A number of Spanish diplomatic missions were made to the United States between 1777 and 1785. One Spanish officer, Juan de Miralles, paid several visits to George Washington, who at that time was serving as general and commander in chief of the colonial armies. De Miralles brought personal gifts for Washington that always included chocolate along with sugar, and occasionally other goods such as wine, almonds, guava jelly, and lemon juice. The future father of America responded with unenthusiastic yet polite thank-you notes ("I am much obliged to you for the present you have sent us....") but made no special remark on the delicacies.

During this time, according to the Journals of the Continental Congress, colonial officers were demanding more provisions. The subsistence money, they claimed, was insufficient, "by the rapid increase of the prices of the necessaries of life." In a resolution to the several legislatures, provisions deemed necessary were outlined: "respectively with the articles at and after the rates following, viz. West India rum two-thirds of a dollar per gallon, Muscovado sugar at half a dollar per pound, coffee at half a dollar per pound, tea at one dollar and two-thirds per pound, and chocolate at half a dollar per pound."

The document further notes that "a Colonel, Lieutenant Colonel, or Chaplain of a Brigade shall be entitled to draw only six gallons of Rum, either

ESTABLISHED IN 1780.

W. BAKER & CO.

PREMIUM

CHOCOLATE

COCOA

BROMA

DORCHESTER, MASS.

OFFICE 26 SOUTH MARKET STREET, BOSTON, MASS.

AND FOR SALE BY ALL THE PRINCIPAL GROCERS IN THE UNITED STATES.

These articles, to which first Premiums have been awarded by the chief Institutes and Fairs of the Union, are an excellent diet for children, invalids, and persons in health; allay, rather than induce, the nervous excitement attendant upon the use of tea or coffee, and are recommended by the most eminent physicians. Being manufactured from Cocoa of the best kind and quality, they are warranted equal, if not superior to any other Chocolates made in the United States, and may be returned if found unequal to the recommendation.

AGENTS.

D. C. MURRAY, New York.	KENNETT & DUDLEY, Cincinnati.	LOCKWOOD, WARD & CO., Troy.
GRANT & TWELLS, Phil'a.	WM. BAGALEY & CO., Pittsburg.	VOSE BROTHERS, New Orleans.
THOS. V. BRUNDIGE, Balt.	WAIT & COATES, Albany.	S. H. HOWELL, Georgetown, D. C.

Baker's high-energy breakfast for frontier living, 1908

four pounds of Coffee or Chocolate, or one pound of tea and twelve pounds of Sugar monthly; A Major or Regimental Surgeon, only four gallons of Rum, either three pounds of Coffee or Chocolate, or three quarters of a pound of tea and eight pounds of Sugar monthly; a Captain, three gallons of Rum and other articles as a Major; and a Lieutenant, Ensign or Surgeons Mate, two gallons of Rum, either two pounds of Coffee or Chocolate, or one half of a pound of tea and six pounds of Sugar monthly."

The American Revolution ended in 1783, but chocolate would not be widely used in the United States for several decades. Because of the high duties imposed on importers by countries that controlled the supply of cacao, as well as that on sugar (which was essential for the enjoyment of chocolate), chocolate would remain a luxury item for some years to come. The War of 1812 with England halted the spread of chocolate in America; Walter Baker & Company, for one, did not operate the mill for two years.

The years that followed are sketchy, but it is evident that other chocolate manufacturers were opening up for business. One Baltimore journal issued a summary statement on mill streams in the area in 1815, noting that among fifty-two flour mills, twenty-seven saw mills, and two paper mills, there was one chocolate mill in operation.

By the mid-1800s, it was as if chocolate had always been with us. In 1869 there were 949 factories making chocolate in the United States, but these were very small operations, many of them apothecary shops that had turned to candy making when the import duties on chocolate were reduced. Mrs. Isabella Beeton's popular book on household management, published in 1861, offered advice on the proper way to serve a box of chocolates, "in an ornamental box, placed on a glass plate or dish." Mrs. Beeton also gave a recipe for hot chocolate in which the dissolved chocolate paste and sugar were poured over the boiling milk-water and stirred over the fire until the mixture was hot and frothy.

In a footnote, Mrs. Beeton wrote that chocolate was seen as a luxury in the United States when it was first introduced "after the discovery of America; but the high duties laid upon it, confined it almost entirely to the wealthier classes. Before it was subject to duty…cocoa plantations were numerous in Jamaica, but that the duty caused their almost entire ruin. The removal of this duty has increased their cultivation."

In the first edition of *The Boston Cooking-School Cook Book,* published by Fannie Merritt Farmer in 1896, there were more than a dozen recipes featuring chocolate, most of which, the author reports, came from Mexico, South America, and the West Indies.

"Cocoa and chocolate differ from tea and coffee inasmuch as they contain nutriment as well as stimulant.... Many people who abstain from the use of tea and coffee find cocoa indispensable. Not only is it valuable for its own nutriment, but for the large amount of milk added to it. Cocoa may well be placed in the dietary of a child after his third year.... Invalids and those of weak digestion can take cocoa where chocolate would prove too rich," wrote Mrs. Farmer.

Although the use of chocolate was expanding, it was still largely seen as a nutritional beverage. "Today it is acknowledged to be a substantial nutrient and analeptic which does not stimulate and exhaust the system like coffee and tea," wrote "a Boston Lady," in *The Dessert Book: A Complete Manual,* written in 1872. The book also warned against adulterations, a common practice during this period, when starches and lentils or lard and mutton-suet were substituted for cocoa butter or when cacao beans were colored with red lead.

By the time one British confectionery industry expert visited the United States in 1920, chocolate factories were "springing up like mushrooms." In the same trade publication, he added that while the Americans "are always up for new ideas, they are mostly 'quantity' specialists." In other words, Americans understood output better than quality. He figured there was a good reason for this: "The American public has never been educated to the standard of chocolate demanded by the European." The war between the palates had already begun.

In a preface to the second edition of his 1912 book on chocolate manufacturing, Robert Whymper wrote: "Chocolates made in America and Europe today are, respectively, as different as chalk from cheese. Perhaps the European taste is that of a *blasé* epicure; perhaps the American palate is uncultured. I will not take it upon myself to pass judgment."

An article in *Candy Factory* magazine in 1923 offered an American opinion on this topic in an article entitled "Is European *chocolate* better than American? The answer is—yes and no." The writer explained that European chocolate was "too carefully refined to suit the average American palate.... The long hot process to which it is often exposed with the intention of developing a caramel flavor is very likely to develop a strong or 'cowy' flavor in the milk."

But beyond taste, something distinct was emerging for chocolate in the New World. One innovation would follow another, and by the early 1900s the world's chocolate industry was huge and growing even bigger. There was an abundance of the raw material to work with, thanks to the rise in the world supply that occurred once cacao cultivation spread to Africa. Production in Africa rose from an average of 79,000 pounds in 1909 to 460,000 pounds by 1934.

By the 1920s, according to historian Ray Broekel, as many as 40,000 different types of candy bars had been created. Relatively few survived, however. Amalgamations, as one industry observer wrote in 1912, were becoming "the order of the day, and science has been called upon by the chocolate industry to assist in the manufacture of a product that was once a luxury...but which is now an expensive necessity." Expensive was a relative term. Cocoa prices would shoot up, stabilize, and shoot up again, but in the meantime, consumption would remain steady. Clearly, when it came to chocolate, most consumers were willing to splurge.

In 1924, a new trade publication for candy retailers was launched with a slogan that read, "Sell Candy Don't Make It." The magazine was promoting the idea that success would belong to the businessman who understood the efficiency of specializing in sales rather than trying to manufacture, package, and sell chocolate, a combination that would not become widespread among small businesses again until the last decade of the twentieth century with the emergence of artisanal choco-late-making.

Regional Chocolate

During World War I, the United States Army commissioned various American chocolate manufacturers to provide twenty- to forty-pound blocks of chocolate to be shipped to bases. The blocks were then chopped up into smaller pieces and distributed to servicemen in Europe. It was just a matter of time before the job of creating smaller pieces fell back to the manufacturers, and that's when the American candy-bar business got its start. When soldiers returned home, they expected to find chocolate candy bars. The war had created a shortage of ingredients but an increase in demand. Chocolate makers experimented and regional companies emerged. Not much seemed to get in the way of making chocolate available to consumers.

One manufacturer was already ahead of the rest of the candy industry. In 1893 Milton S. Hershey, made rich by his Pennsylvania caramel business, attended the Columbian Exposition in Chicago. He became intrigued with a German display of chocolate-making machinery, so he bought some and installed it in his Lancaster factory. By the following year, he had produced his first chocolate bars.

At first, the Hershey Chocolate Company was a mere subsidiary of the caramel business, and in addition to chocolate coatings, Hershey made break-fast cocoa, sweet chocolate, and baking chocolate. By 1900, Hershey had sold the Lancaster Caramel Company for a million dollars, but he kept the choco-late-manufacturing equipment and moved the operation a bit farther west, to the center of Pennsylvania's dairy country. His goal was the mass-production of milk chocolate, and it made sense to be near a constant supply of milk.

An advertisement in a 1921 industry magazine shows a photoengraving of Hershey's new facility with a caption reading simply, "Modern daylight fac-tory, 45 acres of floor space, 8,000 acres of farms." This modest announcement gave only the merest hint of where Hershey was headed, with an entire indus-try after him. Today, Hershey's is the world's largest chocolate manufacturing

A French boy enjoying chocolates given to him by American soldiers

OPPOSITE The Hershey Chocolate Company plant in Pennsylvania, c. 1908

ABOVE Milton Hershey
BELOW Hershey power plant

plant, but it is also unique among American businesses in the way its owner created a community for his workers. As the business did well, so did the town. Hershey built a park, school, churches, stores, and a trolley system.

But Milton Hershey's initial foray into mass-production was primarily to furnish chocolate coatings to candy makers. His business rival, the Mars Corporation, used Hershey's chocolate coatings in the early days. In 1922, however, the Mars father-and-son team, inspired by a trip to a drugstore soda fountain, decided to put the taste of chocolate malted milk in a candy bar, and the result was the Milky Way, which helped make the Mars family one of the wealthiest in the world. Joël Glenn Brenner's book *The Emperors of Chocolate,* published in 1999, is an engaging tale of these two chocolate barons and their vastly different approaches and philosophies.

With such behemoths as Mars and Hershey and their colorful histories, it may be hard to imagine that the candy playground contained any other players. But in 1902, the German company Stollwerck (which had factories in London, Vienna, Kronstadt, and Stamford, Connecticut) was the second-largest chocolate company in the United States. During World War II, however, many

POWER PLANT
Hershey Chocolate Co. Hershey, Pa.

of the Stollwerck factories in Germany were heavily damaged or destroyed, and the firm never fully recovered, although it is still known for having issued pictorial cards and albums with its chocolate products.

There were many other inventive confectioners in the early 1900s, and those that survive today have become icons. Take Tootsie Rolls for instance; they are still made from the same recipe and sell at the original 1896 price—a penny apiece. Tootsie Rolls were created by an Austrian immigrant named Leo Hirshfield, who first made the chewy chocolate candy in a small Manhattan shop and named it for his five-year-old daughter, Clara, whose nickname was Tootsie. The candy's headquarters are in Chicago, with factories in Massachusetts, New York, Tennessee, Mexico, Canada, Eastern Europe, and the Pacific Rim. The company makes more than 49 million Tootsie Rolls every day. (The other famous candy bar named for a child is the Baby Ruth, made first in 1921 by Curtis's Candy of Chicago and given the name of President Grover Cleveland's daughter, not that of a well-known baseball player. In 1964 Curtis went out of business and sold Baby Ruth to Standard Brands, which sold it to Nabisco; in 1990 the candy bar was acquired by the Nestlé Food Corporation.)

The last two miles of the hill were terrible and I said, "Japhy there's one thing I would like right now more than anything in the world more than anything I have ever wanted in my life." Cold dusk winds were blowing, we hurried bent with our backs on the endless trail.

"What?"

"A nice big Hershey bar or even a little one. For some reason or other, a Hershey bar would save my soul right now."

JACK KEROUAC,
The Dharma Bums (1958)

LEFT Some of the classic Mars candy bars

RIGHT Baby Ruth

French chocolate, from *Best Chocolate and Cocoa Recipes,* from Walter Baker & Company, 1931

The Tennessee makers of Goo Goo Clusters can boast that they created the first combination candy bar in 1912, when they mixed peanuts, caramels, and marshmallows and coated the round confection with milk chocolate. The result was advertised as providing "a nourishing lunch" for five cents. This sticky treat is still being made.

And, of course, there was Walter Baker & Company, which in the 1930s offered a full range of products including the result of a collaboration with a cereal company that gave a nod to the health craze of the time. Post's Bran Chocolate, whose slogan reads "Chocolate for the sweet tooth—bran for prevention," is not, however, a confection that survived the tastes of time.

The Baker company, in addition to producing its popular breakfast cocoa, was also a supplier for cooks and printed many recipe pamphlets over the years, stretching the chocolate maker's imagination with a variety of recipes using their products in wafers, cookies, and brownies, as well as in a number of fudge variations. In the early days, as the firm developed, Baker proudly displayed photographs and engravings of their newly acquired machinery. One 1891 booklet illustration of a chocolate machine contained the proud caption: "capacity, five tons of chocolate daily." As new factory equipment was being developed, Baker announced that the firm was ready "to avail itself of every appliance known in modern manufacture" and vowed to make it available for the public to see.

A selection of chocolates available from the Baker company, from *Best Chocolate and Cocoa Recipes,* 1931

OPPOSITE Mars early on understood the importance of prominent in-store displays for its products.

Along with the confections that would over time gain iconic stature in the candy halls of fame were hundreds of small corner candy stores and soda fountains across America. One example of a small candy shop that parlayed its chocolate goods into an empire is See's Candy, which opened its first shop in Los Angeles in 1921; today there are more than two hundred See's shops throughout the western United States.

Seducing Consumers

As business practices became more sophisticated and as a multi-million dollar industry emerged, so did trade publications and organizations, such as the Chocolate Manufacturers' Association, formed in 1923. Confectioners in the early 1900s also had a voice and found a way to communicate marketing strategies, management ideas, and recipes through various publications. There would be ads for a cocoa broker and for, new equipment, such as the 1924

A child's version of paradise: chocolates and television

Northwestern Chocolate Mixer (which worked automatically, turning out batches of one hundred pounds or more at a time). Over the years the advertisements and notices about companies became a kind of yearbook for the candies that would succeed and those that would drop from sight.

The Loft Candy Company in New York published its own newsletter as a way for its shops to communicate ideas and for customers to voice their opinions. A 1918 in-house advertisement announced "A Splendid Opportunity for Some Young Lady." The company was seeking a replacement for a worker who had resigned to marry. She had served as the "Window Demonstrator of Milk Chocolate Fresh Fruits ever since the introduction of this novelty feature." In another issue the company described a series of classes. "Our school for chocolate dippers, bonbon dippers and packers offers unusual opportunities for ambitious young women."

Novelty features were the way to stay competitive in those days, just as they are today (albeit there is more tie-in potential, thanks to the media/entertainment machine). Providing something new and different was one thing, but presenting it in an alluring way was another. A standard feature in one confectioner's journal was a monthly column on window displays. The idea was to teach retailers how to create something so visually arresting that pedestrians and motorists would not only slow down but would actually enter the store.

In the *Candy Kettle,* the Loft Candy Company's newsletter, one Manhattan shop on East Twenty-third Street was applauded for a window setting that featured its product in an "antique Grecian Pottery artistically filled with our various milk chocolates." Another shop window was decorated with red velvet and "an abundance of goldenrod tied with rosettes of wide, red satin ribbon…the lighting effects being red, while the milk chocolates were set off with points of gold foil." During the day it was rather striking, but it was noted that at night, when illuminated by red electric lights it "formed a scene of indescribable beauty."

It was also being noticed during this period that women were emerging as major consumers of chocolates. Chocolate gift boxes were overwhelmingly designed with the feminine market in mind. A woman's place in the factory was in the finishing stages, which required delicate treatment such as ribboning in decorative swirls that distinguished one product from another. The women donned white uniforms and white caps, suggesting a pure and sanitary environment. The men were the jobbers, the salesmen, and, of course, the company executives.

One reader submitted an essay to the *Candy Kettle* that suggested the reason young women could not resist the temptation of window displays was that their displays were as fatal as the siren songs of old. "Nothing, I believe, unless it is a milliner's window in the spring, has a greater attraction for the normally constituted American woman than a tempting display of candy." If the American woman found extra change in her purse as she passed by such a vision of sweets, the writer continued, she would immediately find her way to the shop's door and go in. "If the serpent had tempted Eve with a box of chocolates, she would have gotten more sympathy for her fall among her sisters of today. It really seems sad to think that she 'slipped' and fell for a common everyday Baldwin apple."

It seems appropriate that beautiful chocolates should be placed in beautiful settings, but it could be argued that once chocolate lovers feel that special craving, it probably doesn't matter so much. Nevertheless, presentation can make the ordinary special, not that chocolate is ever ordinary. However, from the very beginning, chocolate was seen as something to be given as a gift, and the packaging of chocolate also became a fine art.

One Short Company History

There will always be a bit of romance associated with the making of chocolate. If we were to examine the histories of all the chocolate empires of today, we would more than likely trace back to one visionary with enough quirky qualities—along with a tasty mixed box of supporting characters—to inspire many books. The story of Crane's Chocolates of Cleveland is a good example. With its blend of characters, ingenuity, commerce, and culture, it is a small slice of Americana.

In 1914 Elbert Hubbard wrote a booklet entitled "A Little Journey to Crane's Chocolate Studio." Hubbard had made a small fortune in the late 1800s writing self-help motivational publications, one of which was the best-selling "A Message to Garcia." He retired to upstate New York to create a utopia inspired by the ideas of William Morris, and he established a center for the Arts and Crafts movement in America. A print shop and bindery, Roycroft Press, was followed by a furniture and metalsmithing shop.

While Hubbard was on the lecture circuit, a fan passed him a five-pound box of chocolates at the Cleveland theater after his talk. "It was the most exquisite box of candy that I had ever thrown my Tungstens on," Hubbard wrote. "The box was a deep red, with jet-black letters, and tied with a broad red ribbon." He continued in this gushy manner to say that Crane's produced the "most beautiful gift boxes of confectionery you ever threw your glimmers on."

The chocolate maker was a former maple syrup businessman named C. A. Crane, who a few years earlier had invented a candy that exists today as a multi-million dollar industry—Life Savers. (He was also the father of poet Hart Crane.) C. A. Crane had created the hard candy as a sideline to his passion, for in the days before refrigeration, chocolate making was a cool-weather job. So the enterprising candymaker, experimenting with a pharmaceutical punch,

CHOCOLATE AMERICANA

In 1922, C. K. Nelson began receiving royalties of about $30,000 a week for his invention of the Eskimo Pie. It had taken nearly four years, however, for him to find a financial backer. According to an article in a 1922 issue of *Western Confectioner,* he was met with a constant rebuff: "Cover ice cream with hot chocolate? Ridiculous!" But Omaha confectioner Russell Stover believed it could be done and put up an undisclosed amount to make the Eskimo Pie a reality.

came up with the colorful rings we know today. In 1913 he sold the formula and trademark for $2,900 and devoted himself to making chocolate.

A few years earlier, Crane had tried to go into business with a Canadian chocolate maker whose goods he found particularly delicious. When the Canadian declined, Crane took a sample of the chocolate, had it chemically analyzed, and began making his own chocolates. This is the candy that Hubbard tasted and raved about in his testimonial tract. To Hubbard's mind, Crane's enterprise embodied everything to be valued in life: good quality with aesthetic sensibilities. What is more, the working environment was also a place of art, "and that is why I think of it as a studio, and not a factory," Hubbard wrote.

This was an artisan at work, not some faceless corporation. Crane's chocolates were not "turned out of a machine, like sausages, at the rate of a ton an hour or so and then dumped higgledy-piggledy into boxes." Crane also understood the importance of packaging. He had been planning with Maxfield Parrish to reproduce the noted illustrator's paintings on the covers of his gift boxes. Parrish had enjoyed great success as a commercial artist, but financially he was in a bit of a slump, and the collaboration with Crane promised to be a lucrative one. In each box was a coupon offering a reproduction of the cover for ten cents, a campaign that proved to be a financial success for both artist and chocolatier. According to Hubbard, Crane's would also be was the first line of chocolates sold by the Chicago-based department store Marshall Field's.

How did it all end? Hubbard drowned off the coast of Ireland when the *Lusitania* sank in 1915, and the Great Depression swallowed up Crane's Chocolates. Hart Crane, the respected young lyric poet, committed suicide in 1932 by jumping off a boat in the Caribbean Sea. Marshall Field's recently made chocolate news when it ceased in-store production of its Frango Mints. And in 2000, a Crane's chocolate box with the Parrish reproduction, "The Garden of Allah" on the cover, sold at auction for $1,265.

New and Improved

The way to survive in the competitive world of confectionery is, as in any other industry, by continuing to create something new. New lines, new flavor combinations, old recipes with new names. Novelty is always the order of the day. Trade magazines in the early days were filled with announcements for new milk chocolates filled with maple cream, butter cream, nougatine, and pineapple. The call to retailers was "Fill your windows with sentiment."

New brands were constantly being invented. A campaign for Dolly Varden Chocolates in 1917 read: "This striking window display card will help you sell Dolly Varden Chocolates. Their fascinating name, superb quality and national reputations assures immediate and constant demand for them."

But chocolate concoctions can also be victim to the tastes of a time. Products that seemed like a great idea to some entrepreneur may not travel well for one reason or another. An example is Benedict's Milk Chocolate Cigarettes, which advertised in the early 1950s with the motto "Just Like Dad's."

In 1979 Adrianne Marcus wrote *The Chocolate Bible,* a dream of a book project that involved driving around the country eating chocolate and compiling a directory of her findings. "During the growing up of America, each town, or almost each town, had its individual candy makers," wrote Marcus. But this had changed radically by 1979. There were fewer hand-made chocolates and plenty of inexpensive mass-produced candy bars. There was also, Marcus reported, a "decline in the art of chocolate dipping." Still, she wrote, there were a good number of great chocolate makers, big and small.

Chocolate making in America seems to be, if not coming full circle, at least facing a new direction. If there is a return to older practices, it is in the making of smaller batches. The word "handcrafted" pops up a lot these days. There appears to be an effort to underscore quality, to strive for premium chocolate, and to define what that means to consumers. But, more important, there seems to be a concern for where the cacao beans actually come from.

Milton Hershey was a visionary. He sold off his lucrative caramel business, but he knew better about chocolate. "Caramels are only a fad. Chocolate is a permanent thing."

> "First as a beverage, then as a sweetmeat, chocolate has steadily worked its way into public favour, and it is safe to say that in no civilised country of the world is the 'Prince of sweetmeats' unknown, and that, wherever civilised man has explored, travelled or sojourned, there may be found a wrapper, yellow, blue, red or white, that once contained a tablet of some well-known brand."
>
> Robert Whymper, *Cocoa and Chocolate: Their Chemistry and Manufacture* (1921)

Growing the Business

In a 1927 trade journal for the candy industry, the headline over a panoramic photograph of a string of railroad cars reads "A Train of Chocolate." The short article that accompanied the picture began by saying that people don't have even the "remotest idea of the magnitude of the candy industry." The average consumer, the journalist continued, believes candy to be something that comes out "of a spotless glass counter, not from a great factory."

Before the industrial revolution, chocolate-making was an artisan's trade, and most of the preparation was done by hand. But as chocolate gained in popularity, chocolate makers devised methods and machines to enable them to make large quantities without sacrificing quality. The invention of the steam engine in 1765 affected virtually every type of industry, including chocolate making. It is believed that the first machines used in the making of chocolate were developed at a factory that opened in 1780 in Barcelona.

A significant milestone in the mass production of chocolate was Coenraad Van Houten's invention of the cocoa press in 1828 and his development of the so-called dutching process to make cocoa easier to dissolve in water. The Swiss inventions of milk chocolate and the conching technique were other important

Chocolatiers are known for their creative promotions. This dress made of chocolate was modeled at a recent trade show.

OPPOSITE All chocolate makers have their secret recipes, which they guard carefully, even today.

steps in the growth of what is now a multibillion dollar industry. However, the most important part of the process—and one that has never been duplicated in a factory—is the production of cacao itself. Scientists and chemists have been unable to produce a palatable artificial chocolate, which means that without *Theobroma cacao,* the chocolate-makers would be truly up a tree. Chocolatiers continue to rely on the tropical growers of this very special plant and on the middlemen who move the crop from one continent to another, a complicated business dependent on such unstable factors as supply, demand, politics, disease, and the weather.

In 1920s the industry was still in its infancy. It is unlikely that anyone other than candymen (a term of the day) or retailers saw the trade journal where the "Train of Chocolate" photograph appeared. That train was destined to be turned into candy bars by the now-defunct Shotwell Manufacturing Company in Illinois, then one of the largest users of chocolate in the country. According to the author of the article, "many such trainloads of chocolate are used each year to make a greater number of train loads of candy bars, which, in turn, provide cash-register music for dealers the country over and unbounded joy to millions of children."

A chemist in a chocolate factory studies the goods.

In 1923, four years before the "Train of Chocolate" article was published, ten American chocolate processors had joined together to establish the Chocolate Manufacturers' Association (CMA) to help deal with the less romantic side of the booming industry, such as politics and economics. Because cacao does not grow in the United States, the American chocolate industry is dependent on imports, and two of the other basic ingredients in candy—sugar and peanuts—are government subsidized, which makes them very costly as well, according to chocolate industry officials. There has not been much unity in the international chocolate industry, and attempts to achieve agreements on world prices usually end in a stalemate.

There has, however, been cooperation in recent years over ecological and scientific research. The survival of cacao is, after all, more than simply a question of cost. The CMA supports a not-for-profit institute that is devoted to scientific research on cocoa and chocolate. Another cooperative effort has been CMA's affiliation with the National Confectioners Association, which was founded in 1984 and now has 270 members, many of them international, which produce more than 90 percent of the chocolate confections produced in the United States. Together, the associations lobby the government to oppose taxes and fees imposed on imported products required for their industry, which generated $22.7 billion in sales in 1998. That's a lot of trainloads of cocoa. The general public, which still may not have an idea of the true size of the chocolate industry, is what keeps it growing, of course. In 1999 each American ate, on average, 11.9 pounds of chocolate.

Schoolboy standing next to his science project, a table piled with the amount of chocolate he will eat in a year

Pricing the Bean

In 1925, a group of five traders opened the New York Cocoa Exchange. Cacao, or cocoa as the financial world calls it, had long been a desirable commodity. Before the exchange was founded, a cocoa merchant simply made a telephone call to buy a boatload of beans, which he would sell to a chocolate manufacturer. As one trade-industry article put it, the exchange made "the orderly marketing of this distant crop...possible." In 1979 it merged with the New York Coffee and Sugar Exchange and is now part of the New York Board of Trade.

The price of cocoa beans hinges on supply. As we know, the cacao tree is strictly a tropical plant, whose crop is affected by weather, disease, insects, poor management, and political and economic conditions in the producing countries. Therefore, as with other agricultural commodities, prices for chocolate have never been stable. Commodity futures exchanges are markets where contracts for the future sale and purchase of commodities are auctioned. The exchanges allow buyers to insure their goods (or hedge) against adverse price moves by offering contracts to speculators who are willing to assume the risk. The market price, therefore, depends not only on the abundance and quality of the worldwide crop but also on economic conditions throughout the world. If the crop is found satisfactory, the grower is paid at the current market price, but since conditions change, the prices are always fluctuating. In 1927 a trade

Beans bagged for shipping

magazine editorial reported on the "the manner in which the cocoa market is being 'manipulated.' The manipulation may or may not be true, though there is no question about the price of cocoa having gone up." The writer called for candy makers to resign themselves because "low-priced cocoa has gone from the market for good."

In the early 1950s, unstable cocoa prices again made headlines. One chocolate company executive blamed the wide fluctuations on insufficient crops and "manipulations by monopolists and speculators." Analyses performed at the time indicated that the world output of cacao had been affected by war and plant disease. Before World War II, the world's cocoa production had reached a record 787,000 tons, but by 1944 it had dropped to 554,000 tons. Shipping was seriously disrupted, and Latin American farmers turned to more lucrative crops to meet war demands. Disease also took its toll; on Africa's Gold Coast, swollen shoot disease killed 20,000 trees in less than six months. In 1989 Brazil was hit with witch's broom (*Crinipellis perniciosa*), another disease affecting cacao trees, and by 1994, its production had decreased by 60 percent. In 1992, Bahia, Brazil, was the world's second largest producer after Ivory Coast, but it has since dropped to eighth place, following Ghana, Malaysia, Indonesia, and Nigeria. About 80 percent of the cacao bean crop in those countries is grown by farmers with plots of about ten acres, most of whom have never tasted chocolate.

Prices today continue to rise and fall as a result of increasingly complicated factors. The industry now has cocoa exchanges in London, Hamburg, and Amsterdam, as well as New York, and traders continue to study the weather and political conditions on an international level. During the spring of 2001, one New York-based trader was looking at rainfall, in particular, because of droughts that were occurring here and there around the world. "This is a critical time," he said. "We have to make sure the cacao trees get enough water." News reports of child labor and slavery in the Ivory Coast and Ghana were also generating news at the Cocoa Exchange in early 2001. Although not completely substantiated, those reports could ultimately create a response that would affect the price of the crop. Chocolate companies creating treats for children don't want to be associated in any way with farms that depend on child labor.

Historically, chocolate companies have tried to control the supply of crucial ingredients by operating their own sugar and cacao farms. Nestlé chose

Fulton, New York, as a site for its factory because of the numerous dairy farms in the area, much as Milton Hershey had done in Pennsylvania. The British confectioner Terry's of York, founded in 1767, began making chocolate in 1886; in the early 1920s the firm purchased a cacao plantation in Venezuela in order to secure a source for their most important ingredient. As the company brochure put it, "Latin America was the source of Criollo, the rarest and most delicately flavored of the many types of cacao bean, and the one on which, above all others, Terry's depended for the individual flavor of their chocolate." But after World War II, the company could no longer afford to manage the plantation. In 1916 Milton Hershey wanted to be sure of a steady supply of sugar, so he purchased a sugar refinery in Cuba and built an electric railroad to service it. As revolution began brewing in Cuba during the 1940s, however, Hershey sold the enterprise to a Cuban company.

The Birth of Big Chocolate

In 1952 a confectionery trade magazine ran a story called "Chocolate Trade's Growth Bright Chapter in History," in which the reporter attempted to trace the development of the chocolate industry. He was frustrated, however, by the lack of information about the history of such "a national institution." For years, he wrote, Hershey was the only chocolate company that had been required to issue industry reports by the Securities Exchange Commission and the New York Stock Exchange. The Brooklyn-based Rockwood, then the second largest American firm in America, though now out of business, had no statistics available. Other big companies discussed in the article were Walter Baker Chocolates in Massachusetts, Wilbur & Ideal and Hooton in New Jersey, and Hershey, Blumenthal Brothers, and Klein in Pennsylvania. Not all of these companies still exist and those that do have been enrobed in other corporate identities. Two of the largest chocolate makers today, Mars and Nestlé, weren't even mentioned.

In both Europe and America, the chocolate industry has become a real melting pot, as big companies eat up smaller ones and large companies are blended into even larger corporations. Nevertheless, some of the oldest small firms can still be found if one probes deeply into corporate histories. For example, the famous French company Menier started in an apothecary shop in 1816, offering chocolate-coated medicine along with "household" chocolate. Like Cadbury and Hershey, Émile-Justin Menier was a visionary when it came to creating a business. Menier purchased cocoa plantations in Nicaragua, kept his own ships, owned sugar houses, and operated a factory in London. In Menier's town of Noisiel, he built hotels for single workers, shops, restaurants, a school, town hall, bank, and model farm. Small houses, each with its own garden, were designed to accommodate two families. In 1860 Menier commissioned the architect Jules

Façade of the Menier "cathedral"

The Swiss firm Cailler, founded in 1819, is now part of Nestlé. Suchard, another old Swiss firm, is now a brand of Kraft Foods.

Saulnier to design a chocolate factory; in 1872, elaborately decorated with ceramic tiles embellished with flower and cacao bean patterns, the factory was so beautiful it was referred to as "the Cathedral." In 1978 the Menier firm merged with the British company Rowntree Mackintosh, and in 1988, the company was bought by Nestlé France, a descendant of the firm established by the Swiss chemist Henri Nestlé, who made the condensed milk that confectioner Daniel Peter had used in 1875 to invent milk chocolate.

Another Swiss confectioner, Charles-Amedee Kohler, had got his start selling ready-made chocolate, but in 1830 he began making his own and eventually

created the first hazelnut chocolate. In 1905 the Kohler firm joined the Daniel Peter company, and they merged with the business started by another pioneer in Swiss chocolate-making, François-Louis Cailler, who opened a chocolate factory on Lake Geneva in 1819. In 1929 Peter-Cailler-Kohler was purchased by Nestlé, now a multinational corporation with factories in many countries.

In 1996 the Belgian chocolate producer Callebaut merged with the French firm Cacao Barry, which supplies chocolate to the food industry. This sounds simple enough, but like the others, it has an interesting lineage. It all started with Philippe Suchard, who opened his first confectionary shop in Neuchâtel,

Van Houten and Bensdorp, two old Dutch firms, have been merged into Barry Callebaut AG, a corporation that operates chocolate-processing plants.

Caley of Norwich has manufactured chocolate in England since 1883.

Switzerland, in 1825. In 1981, Suchard, which had joined with another old Swiss chocolate maker, Tobler, bought Callebaut, which had been first established in 1850 in Belgium and produced its first chocolate candy bar in 1925. In 1983 the Swiss coffee baron Klaus Jacobs bought Tobler-Suchard, and the business became known as Jacobs Suchard, which bought another Belgian chocolate maker, Côte d'Or, in 1987. In 1990, the American firm Philip Morris bought the confectionary division of Jacobs Suchard (for the not inconsiderable sum of $4.1 billion) and now, through its Kraft Foods division, sells chocolate candy under such familiar names as Toblerone, Suchard, and Côte d'Or.

The cocoa-processing, or industrial, division of the Jacobs Suchard firm was acquired in 1990 by another old chocolate company, the Dutch firm Van Houten, which was transferred in 1994 to a new holding company called Callebaut AG. Cacao Barry, which had started in England in 1842, owned processing plants in Cameroon and the Ivory Coast from 1952 to 1965 and in 1985 acquired Bensdorp Chocolate, a Dutch firm. A decade later Cacao Barry merged with Callebaut, and under the name of Barry Callebaut AG, the corporation owns and operates processing plants in Asia, Africa, South America, and Europe.

Even in America, company histories are not simple. Lamont Corliss, established in 1901, had held exclusive sales rights for Peters Milk Chocolate in the United States and Canada since 1902. In 1929, the company was purchased by Nestlé and a few years later changed its name to Nestlé Chocolate Company, Inc. The venerable Baker chocolate factory, purchased by General Foods in 1927, continued to make chocolate at the historic mill along the Neponset in Dorchester, Massachusetts, until 1965, when the operation was moved to Dover, Delaware. The old red-brick plant, the first successful chocolate mill in America, has been turned into condominiums. General Foods was purchased by Kraft in the mid-1980s, and in 1989, the conglomerate became part of Philip Morris, which, as we have seen, owns Jacobs Suchard and other European chocolatiers.

Wilbur, founded in 1884 in Philadelphia, still makes chocolate for confectioners, dairies, bakers, and candy makers, although today the firm is a division of agribusiness giant Cargill, Inc. Ambrosia Chocolate Company, established in Milwaukee in 1894, was purchased by W. R. Grace & Co. in 1964. Grace sold the cocoa subsidiary to grain and livestock feed giant Archer Daniels Midland Co. in the mid-1990s. According to a company press release, "The purchase of Grace Coco—which turns cocoa beans into cocoa liqueur, butter, powder, and chocolate—marks ADM's entry into cocoa processing."

Blommer Chocolate got its start in 1939 by Henry Blommer, Sr., a former partner in Ambrosia. Blommer managed to remain a family-owned business despite Cargill's attempt at a takeover in the early 1990s. Blommer Chocolate is a large American processor of cacao beans and producer of chocolate products, with factories in Illinois, California, and Pennsylvania. Blommer, which reports that it processes more than 100,000 metric tons of cocoa beans every year, recently joined the premium chocolate trend with its Signature Line chocolate and Specialty Cocoas. World's Finest Chocolate, family-owned since 1938, specializes in making candy for fund-raisers. The company has plants in Chicago, Australia, and Canada, as well as a cocoa plantation on the island of St. Lucia and a printing company that makes the company candy wrappers.

A 1902 trade card advertising Tobler chocolates, made in Bern, Switzerland

Frenchman Étienne Guittard came to San Francisco in search of gold, but decided to start a chocolate business instead. Like Valrhona of France, Guittard supplies chocolate for cooks and is still run by family members. Domingo Ghirardelli, an Italian-born chocolate maker also came to San Francisco for the gold rush, but saved his money to start a chocolate business in 1849. In 1998, Ghirardelli was bought by the venerable Austrian firm Lindt & Sprüngli, which had been established in 1845 by confectioner David Sprüngli-Schwarz and his son, Rudolf Sprüngli-Ammann. In 1899 that firm acquired the small but famous chocolate factory of Rodolphe Lindt, who in 1879 had devised the conching technique, which produces a smooth eating chocolate.

For the past thirty years, Mars and Hershey have ruled in the United States; between them the two firms produce eight of the ten top-selling candy bars in the country. And they are practically neighbors. Mars manufactures its chocolate in Elizabethtown, Pennsylvania, just thirty miles from Hershey. American chocolate companies have come a long way since the mid-nineteenth century, when most of the 900 small factories were operated by six people or fewer. The twenty-four cacao bean silos at the Hershey plant can hold up to 90 million pounds of beans. The other giant, Nestlé Chocolate & Confections, produces more than 200 million pounds of chocolate a year at its plant in Fulton, New York.

Small Is also Big

The big may be getting bigger, but the small chocolatier is also on the rise. There is a new appreciation for artisanal chocolates, quality beans, and premium chocolates with a higher cocoa content. Even large chocolate makers are offering premium chocolate. Single-origin chocolate (made with the beans produced in just one country) and organic chocolate (grown without chemicals) are also part of the current trend. Just as wines and coffees have degrees of excellence, so does chocolate. In fact, there is a tasting protocol for chocolate that many gourmets compare to tasting wine: Chocolate is to be eaten at room temperature; its texture, aroma, color, and snap (the clean sound that solid chocolate makes when it is broken) are all to be taken into account. Chocolate must smell good and melt gently in your mouth; remember, one of the wonders of cocoa butter is that it melts at body temperature. Like wine, which is also harvested, fermented, and blended, finished chocolate is often matured for two or three months before sale.

In recent years chocolate has usually been made from a mixture of beans, but the current fashion among chocolatiers is chocolate from a single country, such as Venezuela or Madagascar. Chocolate purists also consider the quality of the three varieties: criollo, forastero, and trinitario. For instance, forasteros of Africa have a strong taste that fades gently, while criollos and trinitarios linger on the tongue. Purists also argue that the mass-production of chocolate,

"I'm the fourth generation in my family to make chocolate. My grandfather's first building was destroyed in the California earthquake in 1906. I remember running around with my brothers in the late 40's and early 50's in the old, dingy factory on the San Francisco waterfront where my grandfather relocated. At the end of the day the aroma of chocolate permeated our clothes. You can't go into a chocolate factory and not come out smelling like chocolate."

GARY GUITTARD,
"The Boss: I'm the
Chocolate Maker's Son,"
The New York Times,
November 29, 2000

Chocolate's exotic origins are part of its international appeal.

like the mass-production of just about anything, results in inferior products. The taste for luxury chocolates in the United States has grown in the last few years, marked by the opening of many mall boutiques across the country during the 1980s by the Belgian company Godiva, which had established its first American shop in 1966.

An editorial in a 1998 issue of the magazine *Chocolatier* read: "All of a sudden 70 percent cocoa solid chocolate bars are the rage. Two years ago you couldn't give them away." The average cocoa content in a basic chocolate bar is about 20 percent, but North Americans seem to prefer a chocolate that is highly sugared

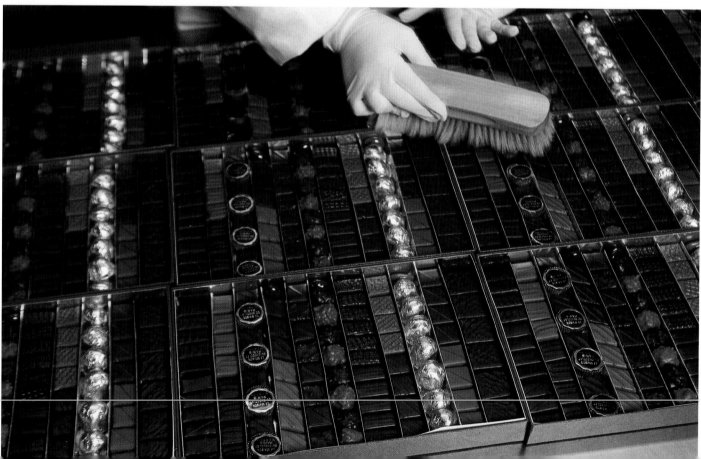

and contains a lot of milk, and English chocolate is not much different. As more and more taste buds are exposed to premium chocolate bars that contain more than 50 percent cocoa solids, there is a growing awareness of the origin and future of chocolate. High-quality beans, described by one industry expert as having a "good fruity, floral flavor," are both born and made. The smaller the farm, the better the chance that the cacao will be superior. And, as we have learned, the smaller the grove and the shorter the distance to the rainforest, the happier the tree.

What is it exactly that makes a premium chocolate premium? The character of cacao beans is influenced by many factors, including soil, climate, and tree variety; and the richness and flavor of good chocolate are affected by the care that farmers give to their trees and beans. Farmers can decide, by the amount of attention they can give their cacao crop, whether they will be producing beans for fine flavor. These high-quality beans, which are grown mostly in Venezuela, Ghana, Ecuador, Trinidad, Java, and Indonesia, make up only 150,000 tons out of 3 million tons grown each year. Big companies, on the other hand, need large, dependable supplies of beans, which will be mixed with so much sugar that the quality is of less importance. Other factors influencing taste, such as fermentation and roasting (it is possible to over-roast), are time-consuming and labor-intensive, whereas shortcuts or oversights can be masked with sugar.

Great chocolate is also the result of a skillful blend of different types of cacao beans. Scharffen Berger, a premium chocolate maker based in northern California, blends about ten or eleven different varieties of beans from different farmers to achieve the desired flavor and body. The company, which started out as a supplier to bakers and candy makers, describes this process as a "fluid and inexact science," mostly because the sources for beans are continually shifting. For instance, the small company began making its high-quality chocolate using mostly beans from Brazil but now uses beans from other areas as Brazil's production declines as a result of disease. In the past, such formulas for blends were well-kept company secrets, but today the goals of the major chocolate firms and the artisanal chocolate makers are so different that such secrecy is no longer necessary.

ABOVE Artisan chocolates

OPPOSITE Chocolate-covered candies

Chocolate as Health Food

Organic chocolate sales were expected to hit $34.5 million in the United States for the year 2000, according to industry sources, thanks in part to the growth of that market. The concept of what constitutes healthful chocolate has expanded to include more than just organically grown cacao. Along with the emerging taste for premium chocolate has come a taste for less sugar. At one time, health-food stores would not touch chocolate bars but offered carob bars instead; now organic chocolate is as widely available in gourmet shops as it is in food co-ops. In 1995, Cloud Nine, a small New Jersey company, introduced the first organic candy bar made in the United States. Today its products share shelf space with, among others, Newman's Own, Rapunzel, and the British company Green & Black's. Most of these companies have more than the health concerns of their consumers in mind. For some, company ideology is in support of the preservation of small-scale cacao farming. Green & Black's chocolate bar Maya Gold, for example, supports fair trade practices for the small cocoa growers in Belize. While there is no legal definition of fair trade, the company's mission is to see that farmers get more money for their product. Green & Black's, for instance, also supports the preservation of the rainforests and believes that if small farmers can make a good living from growing cacao, they will be less inclined toward deforestation for cattle grazing and other agricultural enterprises.

Finding ways to protect the environment while helping people to make a living—known as venture philanthropy—is the goal of some activists. The Nature Conservancy's EcoEnterprises Fund, for instance, has invested in a private company that is working with small cacao farms in Latin America to develop organic chocolate. The fund has helped Organic Commodities Products (OCP), a U.S. company that believes agriculture can be used as conservation. OCP manages a one-million-acre reserve along the Costa Rica and Panama border with habitats ranging from lowland rainforest to subalpine meadows; half of Costa Rica's fresh water originates in the area, which is an important habitat for many bird species. Small-scale farmers work their crops into this environment rather than replacing it, thus sustaining the rainforest, which in turn helps to contain the problems of disease and pests. OCP uses organic cocoa from Costa Rica, Panama, Peru, Ecuador, and Brazil and is involved in the development of organic cocoa in Ghana, Venezuela, and Trinidad as well. Newman's Own Organics chocolate bars are produced from OCP products, and Archer Daniels Midland Cocoa is a contract manufacturer for OCP, producing Guayas Dark Organic Chocolate with beans from Ecuador.

Green & Black's uses organic cocoa from a village in Belize and from a project in Togo to make its chocolate bars. Mascao chocolate bars, which are made by Chocolat Stella, a subsidary of Chocolat Bernrain in Switzerland, use organic cocoa from Bolivia. Rapunzel, based in the United States, is made using organic cocoa from the El Ceibo cooperative in Bolivia.

In the world of high-quality beans there is Hawaiian Vintage Chocolate, started in 1986 by Jim Walsh, a former advertising executive from Chicago. Walsh chose the premium criollo variety and established his plantation, on Kona and Kea'au. The fermented, dried beans are sent to California, where they are made into very high-quality chocolate sold by mail order to professional pastry chefs.

Scharffen Berger began offering its chocolate in 1997, using cacao beans that undergo a thorough fermentation (longer fermentation results in a fuller flavor) and contain a higher percentage of cocoa butter. The small company also uses a vintage roasting machine, which requires someone to watch over the process, tending to the peculiarities of each batch.

Gourmet chocolate providers are not all of recent origin. The French firm Valrhona Chocolates, founded in 1922, still uses the expensive criollo variety of cacao beans. Valrhona names their 70 percent cacao bar Guanaja, after the first European encounter with chocolate (Columbus and the canoe filled with "almonds"). The company considers the bar, created in 1986, "the most intense chocolate available today."

Callebaut, a chocolate company that supplies professional cooks, has been around since 1850 and began producing its own chocolate in 1925. A number of other chocolate makers also specialize in premium chocolate such as couverture (meaning that they supply chocolatiers, pastry chefs, and independent shops with quality chocolate). They operate on a smaller scale than other manufacturers; for instance, they move 10 tons of product per day compared to 100 to 150 tons for a large company.

WHITE CHOCOLATE

White chocolate contains cocoa butter, but no cocoa solids, and chocolate purists argue that the confection should not be called "chocolate" at all. The Food and Drug Administration has yet to create a standard of identity for white chocolate, although the Chocolate Manufacturers' Association has petitioned it to do so.

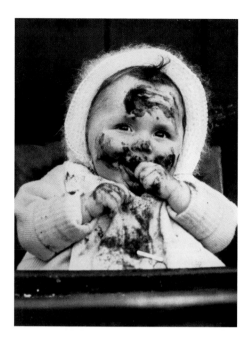

A young chocolate enthusiast

A Matter of Taste and Politics

Ideas about the proper way to prepare chocolate have varied from the very beginning. The Aztecs liked a spicy chocolate beverage, the Spanish a sweetened one. And European chocolatiers have always dismissed American chocolate as inferior. Today chocolate lovers continue to divide themselves into two camps: those who prefer dark, bittersweet chocolate and those who prefer milk chocolate. Chocolate companies cater to both tastes and often develop their own flavors, using a specific type of cacao bean or creating special blends using several types.

In Europe, where the chocolate business is worth about $3 billion a year, a kind of chocolate war has been raging for more than twenty-five years over the definition of "chocolate." The French and Belgian chocolate industries have, with the support of their governments, fought to reserve the term *chocolate* for the product made exclusively with cocoa butter. However, chocolate produced in Ireland, as well as in Britain, Denmark, and Finland, typically contains up to 5 percent of vegetable oils other than cocoa butter. In 2000, the European Parliament adopted a directive (by which individual countries were to pass legislation) authorizing the use of vegetable fats in chocolate: six different types of vegetable fats may legally be used as a substitute for cocoa butter as long as they do not account for more than 5 percent of the final product and the ingredients are clearly labeled.

Chocolate makers who oppose the use of vegetable fats announced in response to the new directive that they would create their own label declaring their products are "made from pure cocoa butter." In a news report one Cadbury official was quoted as saying that the directive was a breakthrough that would "encourage free trade and allow different chocolate-making traditions to co-exist in a market where people can choose." But not all countries see it this way. Spain and Italy were unwilling even in late 2000 to accept the directive and allow the sale of chocolate containing vegetable fat; as a result, they face a formal rebuke from European Union officials.

Chocolate purists, of course, believe a candy bar made with anything other than cocoa butter may not be called chocolate. British milk chocolate has always had a higher milk content than other European products; another proposal offered during the European debate was that those products be labeled "family milk chocolate." At least the European Union did not adopt the Belgian proposal that chocolate made with non-cocoa butter be called "vegelate."

The European chocolate wars have included at least one skirmish that had nothing to do with ingredients. Chocosuisse, the Swiss chocolate trade organization, took Cadbury to court in 1997 to force it to drop its Swiss Chalet chocolate bar complete with a picture of the Matterhorn on the wrapper, because it was not made in Switzerland and was misleading consumers. The argument was that Swiss chocolate indicated a level of unique quality comparable to French champagne and Scotch whisky. Chocosuisse won their case.

There has not been much unity in the international chocolate industry, and attempts to achieve agreements on world prices usually end in a stalemate. There has, however, been cooperation in recent years with ecological and scientific research. The survival of cacao is, after all, more than simply a question of cost.

The marquise de Sevigné (1626–1696) first tried chocolate in 1671 and recorded the event in her famous journal. Years later she would write in a letter to her daughter, "If you are not feeling well, if you have not slept, chocolate will revive you. But you have no chocolate! I think of that again and again. My dear, how will you ever manage?" But not long after, she would write: "I want to tell you, my dear child, that chocolate is no longer for me what it was, fashion has led me astray, as it always does. Everyone who spoke well of it now tells me bad things about it; it is cursed, and accused of causing one's ills; it is the source of vapors and palpitations." She even gossiped about another marquise who "took so much chocolate during her pregnancy last year that she produced a small boy as black as the devil, who died." Chocolate, however, won out in the end. "I have reconciled myself to chocolate. I took it the day before yesterday to digest my dinner, to have a good meal, and I took it yesterday to nourish me so that I could fast until evening: it gave me all the effects I wanted."

A French chocolate company appropriately called Marquise de Sevigné was established in 1898; it produces hazelnut pralines coated with dark chocolate and enclosed in a wrapper with the marquise's face printed on it.

Selling the Product

In the early days, chocolate was subject to seasonal conditions. A 1915 advertisement for a Crystal Chocolate Refrigerator made the point that retailers and manufacturers could keep their chocolate candy trade going all summer if they used a refrigerator. "You need not give up the most profitable part of your candy trade just because the weather gets warm. With this wonderful appliance, the chocolates would be "ice cooled" and kept "in the pink of condition" for only about eight cents a day. Once chocolate makers learned to conquer the temperature, they learned to conquer the seasons. The candy business quickly grasped the idea of using holidays to market their goods. By 1924, chocolate candy makers counted Christmas as one of their best sales times, but another holiday was rapidly becoming lucrative.

"The demand for a special kind of candy known as Easter candies on Easter day has grown to such a volume that manufacturers start to prepare their lines and produce their goods long previous to the Easter season," according to one industry article. And the same kind of thinking was applied to Valentine's Day. Retailers were encouraged to adopt the slogan "Make Candy Your Valentine." In 1999 Americans spent $1.059 billion on Valentine's Day candies, making it the fourth biggest holiday of the year for the candy industry. (Halloween is first, followed by Christmas and Easter.)

In 1893, Chocolat Menier decided to use advertising to promote the brand and settled on the now famous image of a little girl with a long braid holding a chocolate bar in one hand, writing on a blackboard: "Avoid imitations." The French company also chose yellow paper, somewhat revolutionary, to wrap its goods. In 1939 Menier offered dark chocolate tablets that were packaged with stickers and prizes that promoted Walt Disney's new film, *Snow White*. Today, cross-promotions and tie-ins are used ad nauseam, creating a host of collectible doodads for the future. Despite the apparent sophistication (craven or not) of marketing, some blunders have been made. Brenner writes in *The Emperors of Chocolate* how Mars declined an invitation to promote M&M candies in a new science fiction movie. Hershey didn't. When E.T. munched on Reese's Pieces, sales of that peanut butter treat tripled within two weeks of the movie's release.

An early Valentine advertisement

LEFT This "Fabergé egg" was hand-made by John Down, chocolatier for the specialty house of Christopher Norman Chocolates in New York City.

ABOVE Workers making Easter eggs in a candy factory.

In spite of rivalries, disagreements, and international disputes, candy makers always seem to have had one main goal in mind: Come up with a tasty and novel treat and cover it with chocolate. In a 1952 textbook on candy making, the author explains the routine process of making candy as the bones of the industry. "However the bones may acquire flesh as it were, for many of the items and the confections we have already dealt with, can be covered with chocolate: transformed thereby into a prestige class of sweetmeats." In short, chocolate glamorized the goods.

Khuno, the god of storms, destroyed a village with torrential rain and hail because he was angry at the people for having set fire to the forest to clear land for their crops. After the storm, the people found a plant. This was the beginning of the use of cacao.

a Peruvian myth

The Future of Chocolate

Destruction of the tropical rainforest leads to the loss of countless plant and animal species, many of no apparent use to humans and some so commonly used by us that we cannot imagine life without them. Their usefulness to humans aside, each of these threatened species is crucial to the rainforest ecosystem, although in ways not yet completely understood. As the rainforest vanishes, so do our opportunities for scientific research, not only to advance our understanding of this remarkable environment but also to search for new sources of medicinal or nutritional benefit. Because the rainforest is difficult to study, no one can know the extent to which the wild cacao tree benefits from and contributes to the ecological system in which it evolved. However, it seems evident that this tree of great value to humans, like many others in the rainforest, is an essential and integral part of its natural environment, in ways that we may not even recognize. In 1996, for example, a previously unknown species of bird—the pinklegged graveteiro (*Acronatornis fonsecai*)—was found living in the canopy above a cacao grove in Bahia, Brazil. As cacao trees succumb to disease and as the taller trees in the forest canopy are cut for lumber, this bird and many other creatures of the rainforest could lose their homes and disappear.

This white-faced capuchin monkey is an inhabitant of the rainforest.

OPPOSITE The pink-legged graveteiro, a bird that migrates from the north and spends each winter in the branches above cacao trees, was discovered by scientists in 1996.

Slash-and-burn clearing of the rainforest for farming in Equatorial Guinea

A special relationship exists between one of our favorite foods and the rainforest from which it emerged and on which it still depends. If we can understand the link between cacao production and deforestation, perhaps we can participate in securing the future of both the rainforest and chocolate. Cacao has been called a frontier crop, and its cultivation has been driven around the world by the mercantile and colonial interests of European and American businesses. Much of this movement has been caused by the pests and plant diseases that first devastated cacao plantations in the Americas. In the 1980s, an infestation of frosty pod rot decimated Costa Rica's cacao production by 73 percent. Brazil, once the world's largest producer and now second only to Ivory Coast, is again facing a growing threat of witch's broom fungus. Recently, a new species of the fungus that causes black pod disease, a relative of the potato blight, was reported near the border of the Ivory Coast. *Theobroma cacao* is running out of places to go.

Cacao trees are not only victims of the shrinking rainforest; cacao farming itself has actually contributed to deforestation. Plantations devastated by disease or pests are often razed, and because it can take more than five years for

LEFT Deforestation in the Ka Pit Rejang River, Borneo

BELOW Timber harvesting in the rainforest in Malaysia

cacao trees to bear fruit and even longer to attain maximum yields, small farmers cannot afford to invest and wait. One of the worst scenarios is taking place in Africa, where former cacao groves cleared for cattle grazing are turning into grass-covered, treeless savannas. Once that happens, the rainforest is gone for good.

In 1998, scientists, ecologists, cacao researchers, and chocolate industry representatives met in Panama for the First International Sustainable Cocoa Workshop. The gathering, organized by the Smithsonian Institution and supported by M&M/Mars, Inc., was unprecedented. Never before had these participants, representing such disparate interests, met to discuss the one thing they had in common—a concern for the future of chocolate. The focus of the conference was on developing sustainable cacao farming, which means, in part, maintaining a tropical environment, championing an agricultural system that supports cacao grown in a biologically diverse environment, and supporting small farmers.

Many scientists and industry representatives have said that a *New York Times* story on the conference, which reported an impending chocolate shortage within five to ten years, overstated the problem. Yet with 70 percent of cacao coming from West Africa alone, the ease with which diseases travel, and the loss of cacao gene pools, which disappear along with the rainforest, it seems plain that there is reason for concern. Early in 2001, there were record low prices for cacao beans, but this was caused largely by oversupply and does not reflect the fact that chocolate may become more scarce in the future.

Because deforestation means habitat loss for plants, animals, and insects, it is one of the greatest threats to biological diversity, on which our very survival depends. Tropical forests may represent only about 7 percent of the earth's surface, but within those relatively small areas are the most biologically diverse environments in the world. What is in immediate danger of being lost to us forever are the primary gene pools of the wild ancestor trees that contain genetic secrets to such important factors as resistance to disease.

The Ivory Coast rainforest, the world's largest producer of cacao, has experienced some of the highest rates of deforestation in Africa. According to Conservation International, the country lost more than 40 percent of its forest and woodland between 1977 and 1987. Not all of this destruction is the result of logging or mining; some of the destruction has been caused by farmers clearing the forest for agriculture, including cacao cultivation.

One collaborative effort that resulted from the Panama workshop involves plant geneticists of the United States Department of Agriculture (USDA) and researchers from M&M/Mars, who are collecting genetic samples from the tropical forests for the purpose of study.

Cacao's Most Wanted List

Disease and pests have always been a problem for cacao farmers. The chocolate industry estimates that from 35 to 40 percent of the cacao crop is lost each year to disease. *Theobroma cacao* is being stalked by three serious plant diseases—witch's broom, frosty pod rot (*Moniliophthora rorei*), and black pod rot (*Phytophthora spp.*)—all of which attack the pods and destroy the seeds and other parts of the tree.

The cocoa pod borer, or cocoa moth, is a true houseguest pest: it lays its eggs on the pods and the hatched larvae feed off the pods. The cacao pod borer has been squatting recently in Indonesia, where it managed to infect nearly 20 percent of the cacao crop in 1998.

Witch's broom is a fungus that is nearly impossible to control, despite research efforts. It forms tiny spore-producing mushrooms on parts of the cacao tree and these eventually destroy the beans inside the pods. Witch's broom has steadily attacked cacao trees in Brazil, where in just ten years, production of cocoa beans has dropped from 400,000 to 100,000 metric tons. Wild cacao trees in the rainforest do not seem to be as susceptible to the fungus.

Black pod disease will go wherever cacao is grown in the world. The disease is caused by a complex of species of funguslike microorganisms called Phytophthora (the genus name aptly means "plant destroyer"). Black pod will attack all parts of the cacao plant, and farmers experience a major economic loss when the pod is infected. The disease causes a lesion that eventually covers the entire pod, and a diseased pod will turn black and mummify. It can take several days for the seeds inside the pod to be infected, and sometimes they can be harvested in time. But when the disease invades the internal pod tissues, the seeds will discolor and shrivel. Recently, black pod disease has been especially

Birds like these red and green macaws, which live in the rainforest, break into cacao pods to eat the sweet pulp inside and discard the seeds, which drop to the ground to germinate and form new cacao trees.

severe in West and Central Africa; it also destroyed Costa Rica's cacao industry in the 1980s.

Frosty pod rot, another damaging fungus that infects cacao pods, has appeared in Ecuador, Panama, Costa Rica, and Nicaragua. The pathogen spores penetrate the surface of the pods, causing swelling and discoloration before erupting in whitish lesions. The disease can be controlled to some extent by removing infected pods, but there is no affordable fungicidal treatment available. One possible preventive is a matter of biological control, which pits naturally occurring fungal agents (mycoparasites) against the pathogen spores and prevents their dispersal. This technique of managing frosty pod rot is being tested in Peru, Panama, and Costa Rica with fairly good results. Pod loss has been reduced, and yields have increased in previously abandoned cacao plantations.

Plant diseases and pests are not the only problems cacao faces. In Ghana, for instance, cocoa production shifted from east to west as soil fertility declined and trees aged. Small farmers—and most cacao is grown on small farms—don't often have the information and resources needed to manage pest or disease infestations or to understand soil science. With the emerging consensus in the industry that small farms within the rainforest are the best producers of cacao, that support appears to be on the way. In order to be effective, disease control strategies will have to involve governments, small farmers, environmentalists, and the chocolate-manufacturing industry.

Research and Solutions

As research continues on developing biological control for plant diseases, another area of research—a collaboration between plant pathologists from M&M/Mars and the USDA—is focused on developing genetically resistant species of cacao. Corporate and government scientists have been collecting samples from shrinking gene pools in the world's tropical forests. The ecological organization Conservation International supports a concept called "corridors," which would connect land uses of parks and reserves with low-intensity cultivated areas. Small cacao farms placed within patches of forest create a two-way buffer zone. As we have learned, cacao groves that exist next to the forest do almost

A view of the rainforest in Costa Rica

as well as wild trees—meaning that they are less prone to disease and able to produce higher yields. Small farms that grow cocoa are also encouraged to practice inter-cropping with other foods in order to survive economically.

The American Cocoa Research Institute, the research arm of the Chocolate Manufacturers' Association, is funding a project by scientists from Penn State University. (Pennsylvania is the largest chocolate-producing state in the nation, thanks to Hershey.) The researchers have developed a process to clone genetically identical cacao trees from cacao flowers on a farm in the West Indies belonging to the chief executive officer of World's Finest Chocolate. The aim is to enhance plant quality by choosing high-yield, disease-resistant trees.

Allen Young, an expert on cacao pollination, has been working with scientists in Costa Rica on a sustainable forestry experiment. Instead of clear-cutting for timber, only selected trees will be cut, and in their place will be planted cacao trees that can grow successfully in small stands in the forest understory. Agroforestry, which allows farmers to make a living off crops cultivated in the natural forest, is another agricultural system that can help preserve the rainforest.

The Cocoa Research Unit at the University of the West Indies, a British organization, has a project to conserve wild cacao genetic tissue from the South American rainforest. The scientists are paying particular attention to the criollo cacao bean, which is considered nearly extinct in its pure form. The British-based International Cocoa Organization is working with more than a dozen research institutes on numerous conservation strategies, among them the study of cacao. It would be impossible to list the numerous other projects now under way, but chocolate lovers should feel a little more secure knowing that they are out there. The future of cacao depends on this kind of international cooperation between scientists, industry, and government.

Although it appears that the concept of sustainable cacao farming is slowly becoming accepted conventional wisdom, not everyone appears ready to embrace this approach. Hope springs eternal for believers in mega-agribusiness. In 1998, the same year as the Panama eco-chocolate confab, a very different meeting took place in Australia, a conference examining rural industries. One of the papers, "An Australian Cocoa Industry: Turning Problems into Opportunities," examined the reason cacao has been traditionally "a commodity crop of underdeveloped nations." The research, supported by Cadbury Schweppes, Ltd., was looking beyond issues of climate to the possibilities of biotechnology: "Cocoa pods are not able to be shaken from the trees so the focus is on the pod splitting and bean extraction steps." Since labor is very costly in Australia, the author of the paper argued, research should focus on how to mechanize all the stages of cacao harvesting.

Cacao has been a boom-and-bust crop, between disease and other complicated issues involving price controls, government policy, and oversupply, so another goal of disease and pest management is to help stabilize the supply of cacao beans on the global market. At issue is how to plant cacao in a way that can have both an environmental and economic value, how to help humans to make a living while protecting the forests. Generating political support from national governments is crucial in supporting sustainable cacao programs.

One of the missions of the World Cocoa Foundation, formed by the American Cocoa Research Institute, is to get the information from all this research activity out to the farmers and to help them survive economically. A foundation report states: "Small farmers are at the heart of sustainable cocoa growing. Today five to six million farmers, many of whom live in poverty, grow more than 85 percent of the world's cocoa. Each farmer generally owns two and a half to five acres of land and grows about 1,000 cocoa trees."

Fear of a chocolate shortage has been a stimulus for industry and government to rethink how cacao is grown, to consider the ecology of *Theobroma cacao* and the fate of the people who grow it. The cultivation of cacao got its start in Mexico, where production is now minimal. It cannot afford to lose any more ground.

The Panama conference provided a springboard for further collaboration between industry and government, environmental organizations and businesses. Gradually, all of these groups are recognizing that it makes sense, for the future of chocolate, to preserve a system of agriculture that has been around for thousands of years and that in doing so, they can keep an endangered environment intact.

It is possible that chocolate may be a crucial ingredient in the fight to save the world's rainforests.

A CHOCOLATE TIME LINE

A.D. 600 The Maya establish the earliest known cocoa plantations in the Yucatán.

1200 Aztecs begin their rule Mexico, demanding tributes of cacao, among other products, from conquered territories.

1502 On his fourth voyage to America, Columbus captures a Maya trading canoe in Guanaja and finds in the cargo "almonds" that appear to be used as a currency. Columbus's son describes how, when beans were spilled, the Maya scrambled after them "as if their eyes had dropped out of their sockets."

1513 Hernando de Oviedo y Valdéz, who traveled to America as a member of an expedition, reports that he bought a slave for one hundred cocoa beans.

1519 Hernán Cortés establishes a cocoa plantation in the name of Spain for the cultivation of "money."

1528 Cortés returns to Spain from Mexico with cocoa beans and the utensils necessary for their preparation.

1552 The first known illustration of a cacao tree is made for an Aztec herbal, called the Badianus Manuscript, composed by two Aztec students at the College of Santa Cruz at Tlaltelco, Mexico City.

1560 Criollo cacao from Venezuela is planted in Indonesia by Dutch colonists.

1569 Pope Pius V finds chocolate so unpleasant he declares that "this drink does not break the fast." Debate within the church, however, continues.

1575 Milanese historian and traveler Girolamo Benzoni publishes his *History of the New World,* in which he calls Mexican chocolate "more a drink for pigs than a drink for humanity." During a wine shortage, however, Benzoni tired of drinking water and found that the bitter chocolate "satisfies and refreshes the body."

1585 The first shipment of cacao beans from plantations established in the Americas is delivered to Spain.

1606 Italian businessman Francesco d'Antonio Carletti visits a cacao plantation in Central America, where he observes methods of cultivation and production. He returns to Italy and writes a report on chocolate for Ferdinand I de' Medici, the Grand Duke of Tuscany.

1609 *Libro en el cual se trata del chocolate* is published in Mexico, probably the first book devoted entirely to the subject of chocolate.

1615 The Spanish princess Anne of Austria marries Louis XIII and introduces the drinking of chocolate to the French court, along with other Spanish customs.

1648 Thomas Gage, an English Dominican friar who visited Cortés in the New World, reports on the uses of cacao and chocolate in his book *A New Survey of the West Indies.*

1655 Jamaica is taken from Spain by England and becomes England's main source of cacao.

1657 A Frenchman opens a London shop offering "an excellent West India drink, called Chocolat."

1661 The French medical establishment endorses the use of chocolate.

1662 Cardinal Brancaccio settles the protracted ecclesiastical debate on the use of chocolate during Lent by pronouncing "Liquidum non fragit jejunum" (Liquid does not break the fast.).

1670 Pedro Bravo de los Camerinos, a Spanish helmsman, retires from explorations and long voyages and settles in the Philippines to establish a cacao plantation.

1677 Brazil establishes its first cacao plantations.

1680 British royal physician Sir Hans Sloan blends chocolate with milk for use as a medicinal beverage. As physician to the governor of Jamaica, he observed the locals drinking the bitter chocolate, which he improved by heating it and adding milk and sugar. Sloan's botanical specimen collection, which included cacao beans and leaves, was the foundation for the Natural History Museum in London.

1684 France conquers Cuba and Haiti and start cacao plantations in order to assure a supply of beans for the French market.

1693 White's Chocolate House established in London (and survives today as a gentlemen's club).

1704 Frederick I of Prussia imposes a tax on chocolate to restrict the importation of foreign products. Anyone who wishes to import chocolate must pay for a permit.

1720 Coffee-houses in Florence and Venice begin to offer chocolate.

1732 Frenchman Monsieur Dubuisson invents a table for grinding cacao that is heated underneath to hasten the process.

1746 Cocoa Tree, a chocolate house and Tory club, opens in London.

1750 Henri Lekain blends chocolate with coffee, a drink that Voltaire takes daily.

1753 Swedish naturalist Carolus Linnaeus assigns the classification *Theobroma cacao* to the chocolate tree.

1765 Walter Baker & Company opens the first chocolate mill in the United States.

1773   A guild of chocolate grinders is formed in Madrid with more than 150 members.

1780   The first factory using machines to make chocolate is established in Barcelona.

1795   J. S. Fry & Sons in England grinds cacao beans using steam power.

1800   Debauve & Gallais, pharmacists to King Louis XVI of France, produces medicinal chocolates. In 1819 the firm opens in Paris a chocolate shop that is still in operation.

1810   Venezuela becomes the world's leading cacao producer, supplying half the world's requirements.

1819   François-Louis Cailler opens the first chocolate factory in Switzerland after studying in Italy.

1828   Dutchman Coenraad Van Houten develops a cocoa press, which extracts cocoa butter from the liquor, producing a cake of cocoa. He follows up this invention with the "dutching" process, in which alkali is added to the acidic cocoa powder, mellowing the flavor and enabling it to be mixed easily with liquids.

1832   Franz Sacher, 16-year-old royal pastry chef in Austria, creates the famous sachertorte, a rich chocolate cake covered with apricot preserves and chocolate glaze.

1845   David Sprüngli-Schwarz and son Rudolf Sprüngli-Ammann open a confectionery shop in Zürich.

1847   J. S. Fry & Sons make a "chocolate bar" for eating.

1854   Cacao cultivation is established in Fernando Pó, an island off the coast of West Africa.

1852   Domingo Ghirardelli, an Italian immigrant, opens a chocolate factory in San Francisco.

1853   John Cadbury's firm, founded in 1824, is chosen to be the purveyor of chocolate to Queen Victoria.

1864   Jean Tobler of Bern, Switzerland, begins production of chocolate confections.

1868   Étienne Guittard establishes a chocolate business in San Francisco after studying in France.

1875   Swiss inventor Daniel Peter creates milk chocolate using Henri Nestlé's condensed milk product.

1879   Rodolphe Lindt of Switzerland invents conching, a process that creates a smoother-eating chocolate and revolutionizes chocolate making. The process is still used today.

1879   The first cocoa trees are planted in Ghana, which becomes a world leader in cacao production.

1894   Pennsylvania candymaker Milton Hershey establishes a chocolate company to coat his caramels; he also creates the first Hershey bars.

1907   Hershey introduces Kisses.

1911   Mars chocolate company opens in Tacoma, Washington. Callebaut begins producing chocolate bars in Belgium.

1912   Goo Goo Cluster, candy bar that combines milk chocolate, marshmallow, caramel, and peanuts in Nashville. The Whitman's Sampler, a box of various types of chocolate confections, is created in Philadelphia.

1917   The Clark Bar is created in Pittsburgh.

1921   Bendicks opens in London selling the Bittermints, which are still popular today. Peter Paul Halijian of New Haven, Connecticut, invents the Mounds bar.

1923   Yoo Hoo chocolate drink is invented by Nataled Olivieri, a New Jersey fruit beverage businessman. Mars, founded in Tacoma, Washington, in 1911, invents the Milky Way candy bar, and Russell Stover opens a shop in Kansas.

1925   The New York Cocoa Exchange, modeled after the Chicago Board of Trade, opens to sell cocoa futures. In 1979 the exchange joins the Coffee and Sugar Exchange.

1929   Jose Rafael Zozaya and Carmelo Tuozzo establish the El Rey chocolate company in Venezuela.

1930   Mars introduces the Snickers bar. Ruth Wakefield invents chocolate-chip cookies at her Massachusetts inn. When she ran out of Baker's chocolate, Wakefield broke up a bar of Nestlé semi-sweet chocolate, thinking it would blend with the dough to make chocolate cookies. Her miscalculation became the famous Toll House Cookie. When Nestlé began to produce small chunks of chocolate, they printed the Toll House Cookie recipe on the package.

1939   Chocolate Ibarra established in Guadalajara, Mexico, produces small cakes of cocoa for the making of hot chocolate. The product, which contains cinnamon, reflecting Spanish influence in taste, is still made today.

1967   Dilettante Chocolates opens in Seattle with old family recipes of owner Dana Davenport, whose great uncle had been official chocolatier to Tsar Nicholas II.

1996   Scharffen Berger Chocolate Maker, founded in Berkeley, California, offers its first products for cooks, including a bittersweet chocolate with 70 percent cocoa.

1998   Lindt & Sprüngli acquires Ghirardelli Chocolate Company, combining three venerable chocolate firms dating back to the nineteenth century.

ACKNOWLEDGMENTS

Chocolate could not have been written without the support of many people. I would like to thank my editor, Barbara Burn, at Harry N. Abrams, Inc., and Sophia Siskel of The Field Museum for allowing me to work on such a fun project. I am grateful to many individuals of various libraries and institutions for answering a multitude of questions, including Allen Young; Rosa Perelmuter, Associate Professor of Romance Languages at the University of North Carolina, Chapel Hill; Dr. Margaret Griffin of the Nightingale Project; David Stuart of the Peabody Museum at Harvard University; Dan Morgenstern of the Jazz Studies Institute at Rutgers University; Howard Shapiro at M&M/Mars, Inc.; John Buchanan of Conservation International; and I. Russell Greenberg, director of the Smithsonian Migratory Bird Center. My thanks go also to staff members of the Jefferson Library at Monticello, the Hispanic Society of America in New York, the John D. Rockefeller Jr. Library at Colonial Williamsburg Museum, the Philadelphia Museum of Art library, the Smith College libraries, the Schlesinger Library at Radcliffe, and the New York Public Library. I am grateful as well to Michelle Zackheim, Charlie Ramsburg, Iwona Biedermann, Laura Husar, and Robert Brady for the support of friendship—from housing me while I was on library research trips to providing emergency packages of chocolate during deadline crises.

RUTH LOPEZ

The Field Museum is delighted to co-publish *Chocolate: The Nature of Indulgence* with Harry N. Abrams, Inc., and to present audiences throughout the United States with an exhibition devoted to one of life's sweetest indulgences.

Several individuals must be acknowledged for their role in both the exhibition and the book. Anamari Golf, Exhibition Developer at The Field Museum, led the content-development process for the exhibition, reviewed the manuscript of this book, wrote illustration captions, and supervised the selection and acquisition of photographs for both the book and the exhibition. Lori Walsh, Shelley Ulrich, John Weinstein, Virginia Trice, and Carol Parden also provided content and photography support.

Field Museum research staff contributing to the development of this project include: William Burger, Curator Emeritus of Vascular Plants, Department of Botany; Gary Feinman, Curator of Mesoamerican Archaeology and Ethnology and Chair, Department of Anthropology; Jonathan Haas, MacArthur Curator of North American Anthropology, Department of Anthropology; Sophie Twichell, Environmental Conservation Programs Manager; and Gretchen Baker, former Environmental Conservation Programs Research Assistant.

We owe special thanks to the National Science Foundation, which generously supported the "Chocolate" exhibition.

SOPHIA SISKEL
Director, Exhibitions
The Field Museum

BIBLIOGRAPHY

Amado, Jorge. *The Violent Land,* translated from the Portuguese by Samuel Putnam. New York: Morrow Avon, 1988

Brenner, Joël Glenn. *The Emperors of Chocolate: Inside the Secret World of Hershey and Mars.* New York: Random House, 1999

Brillat-Savarin, Jean Anthelme. *The Physiology of Taste: Or, a Meditation on Transcendental Gastronomy* (1825), translated from the French by M. F. K. Fisher. Reprint edition, Washington, D.C.: Counterpoint Press, 2000

Camporesi, Piero. *Exotic Brew: The Art of Living in the Age of Enlightenment.* Cambridge, England: Polity Press, 1994

Clarence-Smith, William Gervase. *Cocoa and Chocolate, 1765–1914.* Revised edition, London: Routledge, 2000

Coe, Sophie D., and Michael D. Coe. *The True History of Chocolate.* London and New York: Thames & Hudson, 1996

Desaulniers, Marcel. *Death by Chocolate: The Last Word on a Consuming Passion.* New York: Rizzoli, 1992

Heatter, Maida. *Maida Heatter's Book of Great Chocolate.* New York: Random House, 1983

Leon-Portilla, Miguel, ed. *The Broken Spears: The Aztec Account of the Conquest of Mexico.* Boston: Beacon Press, 1962

Malgieri, Nick. *Chocolate: From Simple Cookies to Extravagant Showstoppers.* New York: HarperCollins, 1998

Prescott, W. H. *The History of the Conquest of Mexico* (1843). New York: Modern Library, 1931

Smith, Nigel J. H. *Tropical Forests and their Crops.* Ithaca, N.Y.: Comstock Publishing Associates, 1992

Weil, Dr. Andrew: *From Chocolate to Morphine.* Revised edition, Boston: Houghton Mifflin, 1998

Young, Allen M. *The Chocolate Tree: A Natural History of Cacao.* Washington, D.C.: Smithsonian Institution Press, 1994

EDITOR: Barbara Burn
DESIGNER: Lindgren/Fuller Design

This book is published to accompany an exhibition held at The Field Museum, Chicago, from February 14 through September 8, 2002. The exhibition and its national tour were developed by The Field Museum, Chicago.

Library of Congress Control Number: 2001097226
ISBN 0-8109-0403-9 (Abrams: hardcover)
ISBN 0-8109-2442-0 (museum: paperback)

Text copyright © 2002 Ruth Lopez
Illustrations copyright © The Field Museum, Chicago

Published in 2002 by Harry N. Abrams, Incorporated, New York
All rights reserved. No part of the contents of this book may be reproduced without the written permission of the publisher.
Printed and bound in Italy
10 9 8 7 6 5 4 3 2 1

Harry N. Abrams
100 Fifth Avenue
New York, N.Y. 10011
www.abramsbooks.com

Abrams is a subsidiary of

LA MARTINIÈRE
GROUPE

page 1:   Suchard trade card, c. 1895
page 2:   The tempering process
page 4:   Drying cacao beans, Ivory Coast

Hershey Kisses is a registered trademark of the Hershey Foods Corporation.

M&Ms is a registered trademark of Mars, Incorporated.

PHOTOGRAPH CREDITS

AKG London: pages 1, 74, 114 (right), 119 (right); Allen M. Young and the Society of American Archaeology: page 14; Alvaro Deleiva: page 10 (left); American Museum of Natural History: page 33 (left bottom) photo by John Bigelow Taylor; Art Archive: pages 35 © Mireille Vautier; 114 (left), Museum für Gestaltung, Zurich; Art Resources, N.Y.: pages 34 © Schalkwijk/National Palace, Mexico City; 46 © National Museum of History/Giraudon; 51 Chateaux de Versailles et de Trianon, France; Bodeleian Library, Oxford University: page 31; Bridgeman Art Library: pages 41 (left bottom) British Embassy, Mexico City; 54 Château de Versailles; 58 Philadelphia Museum of Art; British Museum, London: page 56; Bruce Coleman, Inc.: pages 10 (right top) © David Madison; 20 © Ralf Astron; 135 © John Guistina; Christopher Norman Chocolates: page 127 (left); Corbis: pages 57, 89 Bettmann; David Sieren: page 13 (top); Corbis Sygma: pages 15 © Paulo Fridman; 26 (left top and right top), 27 (right top), 120 (both) © Michel Setboun; 107 © Julien Hekiman; 108 © E. Preau; 125 © Bernard Annebique; Denver Museum of Nature and Science: page 39 Dagli Orti Alfredo/ Per I Beni-Artistici E. Storici, Florence; Field Museum: pages 11, 48 (left bottom) © Teresa Murray; 40 (left bottom) © 2001 J. Weinstein A114059 2c; 44 © 2001 J. Weinstein 114060 2c; 87, 97 (left bottom middle) courtesy Fred Rodriguez; George R. Gardiner Museum of Ceramic Art, Toronto: page 50; Getty Images: pages 6, 49 (right top), 80, 84, 85, 94, 100, 109, 124, 127 (right) Hulton Archive; pages 77, 78, 113 © Roger-Viollet; 121© James LeGoy; Hershey Community Archives: pages 95, 96 (left top); Jaime Biondo: page 93; Justin Kerr: pages 32, 42; Kobal Collection: page 59 (right top) © David Appleby/Fat Free Ltd/Miramax; Kunsthistorisches Museum, Vienna: page 52 (right bottom); Magnum: page 76 © Ian Berry; Mars, Incorporated: pages 97 (left bottom), 99; Mary Evans Picture Library: pages 23 (left bottom), 25, 41 (right top), 43, 52 (left top), 53, 59 (left bottom), 60 (both), 61 (both), 68, 72, 73, 90, 102, 106, 115 (both), 117, 119 (left), 126; Minden Pictures: pages 8, 129 © Gerry Ellis; 133© Frans Lanting; Museo de America, Madrid: page 28 photo by Joaquin Otero; Museu de ceramica, Barcelona: page 48 (right top); National Archaeological Museum of Guatemala: pages 3 (far right), 29; National Museum of Natural History/Smithsonian Institution: page 18 (left top) © Chip Clark; Nestlé France: page 24; Newberry Library, Chicago:pages 9, 36, 38 (left bottom); NGS Picture Collection: pages 33 (right top), 37 © George F. Mobley; Odyssey, Chicago: page 38 (right top) Robert Frerck; Olsson-Baber Photography: pages 17, 18 (right bottom), 21, 22 (both), 23 (right top), 40 (left middle), 47 © Mary Baber; 40 (left top) © Russ Olsson; Organic Commodity Products, Inc.:page 19 (left top); Panos Pictures: pages 3 (far left), 12 (left middle) © Jeremy Horner; 13 (right bottom) © Jim Holmes; 16, 130 © Sean Sprague; 131 (left top) © Tony Dallios; 131 (right middle) © Fred Hoogevorst; Paul K. Donahue: page 128; Peter's Chocolate: page 2; Photo Researchers: pages 3 (second from right); 103 © Catherine Ursillo; 12 (right top) © Kjell B. Sandved; 19 (right bottom) © Dr. Morley Read/SPL; 110 © Ronny Jaque; PhotoDisc: pages 3 (second from left), 26 (right bottom); Richard Nowitz: page 27 (left top); Staatliche Kunstsammlungen, Dresden: page 86; State Hermitage Museum, Russia: page 49 (left bottom); Victor Englebert: page 70; Wolfgang Kaehler: pages 26 (left bottom), 27 (left bottom); Woodfin Camp & Associates: pages 4–5, 75 © M & E Bernheim; 27 (right bottom) © James Wilson

WOODBRIDGE TOWN LIBRARY
10 NEWTON ROAD
WOODBRIDGE, CT 06525